A truly gripping saga. Powerful, compelling, and disturbing. The story of what an extraordinary lawyer—moved by faith, dedicated to his clients, and committed to justice—went through to try to hold GM accountable.

—Arthur Bryant, chairman emeritus, Public Justice

This story is about everyday decisions made within corporations that can lead to human tragedy and what it takes to stand up and fight for change.

—Sean Kane, founder and president,
Safety Research and Strategies

The next time you hear someone speak ill of a lawyer or laugh at a lawyer joke, tell them about Lance Cooper and Brooke Melton. Lance is a modern-day warrior against injustice.

—Governor Roy E. Barnes

This is the story of a true American hero, Lance Cooper, who, armed with his brain and law license, uncovered the ugly underbelly of corporate exploitation of the American consumer.

—Robin Frazer Clark, fiftieth president
of the State Bar of Georgia (2012–13)

Cobalt Cover-Up is the real-life story of a tenacious trial lawyer who refused to take no for an answer and relentlessly used the tools of our civil-justice system to obtain justice for a family determined to learn what killed their daughter. In doing so, together they uncovered a deadly secret that a car manufacturer was hiding from the American public, a secret that could have killed scores of other Americans.

—Bill Clark, political affairs director, Georgia
Trial Lawyers Association (2002–19)

While this book is undeniably about corporate corruption, it is more about the love that Ken and Beth Melton had for their daughter, and their drive, alongside their compassionate and driven attorney, Lance Cooper, to prevent corruption from resulting in future tragedies.

—Cory Phillips, principal, Forge Consulting LLC

I wholeheartedly endorse Lance Cooper's book. Readers of *Cobalt Cover-Up* will learn in graphic detail how important our judicial system is for the American people.

—Jere L. Beasley, founder, Beasley Allen Law Firm

This book truly gripped me as I read it from start to finish in one session, broken only by a night's sleep. May it spur us all to prepare for that day when we will individually stand and give account of ourselves before our judge, the Lord Jesus Christ.

—Rev. Dr. Kevin J. Bidwell, minister,
Sheffield Presbyterian Church, England

Lance's relentless pursuit of the truth is inspiring. Not only is Lance one of the most skillful lawyers I know, I've never seen anyone fight harder for his clients.

—Ben Persons, The Persons Firm, LLC

COBALT
COVER-UP

The Inside Story of a Deadly Conspiracy
at the Largest Car Manufacturer in the World

LANCE A. COOPER
WITH MARK TABB

ZONDERVAN BOOKS

Cobalt Cover-Up
Copyright © 2020 by Lance Cooper

Requests for information should be addressed to:
Zondervan, 3900 *Sparks Dr. SE, Grand Rapids, Michigan* 49546

Zondervan titles may be purchased in bulk for educational, business, fundraising, or promotional use. For information, please email SpecialMarkets@Zondervan.com.

ISBN 978-0-310-35626-4 (hardcover)
ISBN 978-0-310-35628-8 (audio)
ISBN 978-0-310-35627-1 (ebook)

Cover design: Curt Diepenhorst
Cover photo: Josh Meister Photo
Interior design: Denise Froehlich

Printed in the United States of America

19 20 21 22 23 24 LSC 10 9 8 7 6 5 4 3 2 1

For my wife, my children,
and my grandchildren.
And for Brooke, who should
still be with us today.

CONTENTS

PROLOGUE

Divine appointments rarely announce their arrival ahead of time. Only in retrospect do we see defining moments. Luke 17:10 says, "So you too, when you do all the things which are commanded you, say, 'We are unworthy slaves; we have done only that which we ought to have done'" (NASB).

I think of that verse a lot when I look back on the first time Ken and Beth Melton walked into my cramped office in Marietta, Georgia. More than a year passed before I grasped the magnitude of their case. Even more time went by before I understood its implications went far beyond a lawsuit. The importance of this case came not through the size of the settlement or even the headlines generated.

Psalm 103:6 says, "The LORD gives righteousness and justice to all who are treated unfairly" (NLT). "Treated unfairly" grossly understates what happened to Ken and Beth's daughter Brooke at the hands of a corporation that placed profit before people's lives and then did its best to keep the truth from ever seeing the light of day.

Jesus said a day is coming when he will make sure secrets "whispered behind closed doors will be shouted from the housetops for all to hear" (Luke 12:3 NLT). Little did I know when I first met Ken and Beth Melton that God would use this case as his megaphone to do just that. So many "coincidences" had to fall into place for this case to reach its result, so many ifs had to come together that only God could have orchestrated the chain of events which started with that first meeting. If an insurance company had come to a timely settlement with accident victims, and if a lawsuit had not been threatened (yet never filed), and if an inspection of a vehicle had not been requested, and if someone had not referred Ken and Beth to me, and if and if and if, then the truth never would have come to light of how General Motors chose to risk people's lives rather than spend less than a dollar per car to fix a defect they covered up for more than a decade.

I cannot take credit for being the one who finally discovered the Cobalt cover-up. God's hand of providence directed me down this path. The God of justice used Brooke Melton's case to produce answers not only for her mom and dad but for all the families who'd suffered a similar loss. I just happened to be the one God chose to be the catalyst for bringing this massive corporate fraud to light. I thank him that he did.

CHAPTER 1

The Nightmare That Refused to End

Ken and Beth Melton had the look of two people who wished they were anywhere else when they walked into my office for the first time on February 8, 2011. As a trial lawyer who represents clients in catastrophic injury and wrongful death cases, I see that look often. I never get used to it. The day I do is the day I need to change careers.

"Is that your family?" Beth asked as she and Ken took their seats across from me. Photographs of my wife and children covered the wall behind me.

"Yes. That's my wife, Sonja, and our five kids, Rachel, Rebekah, Michelle, Asa, and Aaron," I replied.

"They're lovely," Beth said.

"Thank you," I said. "They keep me busy."

"I know how that can be," Ken replied. "We have, uh, had, two daughters. Our oldest . . ." He couldn't finish the sentence.

"Why don't you tell me about her," I said, trying to ease the moment.

"Brooke was twenty-nine when she . . . at the time of her accident," Ken said. "We were so proud of her. She was a nurse over at West

Atlanta Pediatrics. Very independent, but you know, still a daddy's girl. Made all her own decisions, but she'd call me for advice sometimes on dad things, like repairs to her apartment or her car." He paused.

"My girls do the same thing," I said. "You want them to be independent, but it feels good when they call and need you. I am very sorry for the loss of your daughter. If you can, will you tell me what happened the night of Brooke's crash?"

Ken gathered himself. Nearly a year had passed, but his and Beth's grief still felt raw. Ken seemed more agitated, like talking helped him work through what he was feeling. Beth settled back into her chair, quiet, like she could hardly bear to revisit her daughter's death even though she knew she had to.

Ken handed me a document. "This is a copy of the police report," he said. I looked it over as he continued, "It was her birthday, March 10, last year. She had a date with her boyfriend after she got off work. It had rained pretty much all day, but it had slowed down a lot by the time she got off work that night. So Brooke was driving her Cobalt down Highway 92, a two-lane road, when she lost control of her car as she came down a hill. Her car began sliding and crossed over into the other lane, where the oncoming car struck her on the passenger side. Her car then went off the road and down into a creek by the side of the road. By the time the hospital called us, Brooke was . . . she was, uh . . . she was already gone."

"I am so sorry," I said. Those words never seem to be enough. Even though I've worked with many grieving parents, going back to the first case I ever took to trial, I had no idea what the Meltons were experiencing. Even so, sitting with them, listening to their story, I could not help but put myself in their shoes and wonder what I would do if the hospital called to tell me my oldest child had been lost in an accident. I do not know how parents move forward with life after that. I am always amazed that they do.

I scanned the police report. Under "Cause of Accident" were the words "Driver error: Driving too fast for conditions."

"I didn't believe the report's conclusion then and I still don't now," Ken continued. "It says the wreck was Brooke's fault. I don't buy that. Brooke was a very cautious driver. She'd never had an accident before. Never even gotten a ticket. It's not like her to take unnecessary chances. I know it rained that day, but witnesses said it was only a drizzle at the time of the accident. And it's not like she had never driven in the rain before." Ken's emotion stopped his words. I glanced over at Beth. She tried hard to keep her emotions in check but was losing that fight.

"And you are here because your insurance company now wants to inspect the Cobalt?" I asked.

"Yes," Ken said. "Officially the wreck was Brooke's fault, but within a few weeks after her death, we received a recall notice from GM." Ken handed me the recall notice. It was for the electronic power steering on Brooke's Cobalt.

"If the power steering went out, wouldn't that be enough to make someone lose control of their car?" Ken asked.

I read the notice before I answered his question. A couple of sentences jumped out at me. At the bottom of the first paragraph, I read, "If power steering assist is lost, it may require greater driver effort at low vehicle speeds, for example, below 15 mph (25 km/h). *Unless the driver compensates for this additional effort, it may increase the risk of a crash*" (emphasis added). This mixed message caught my eye. The problem was supposed to manifest itself only at low speeds, and yet it also said it could contribute to a crash. Low speeds and accidents do not go together. I'd read enough of these notices to know there may well be more to this than met the eye.

"I'm not a mechanic, but I agree it may be a question worth looking into," I said. "To your knowledge, had she ever had any problems with her power steering before?"

"No. But the recall makes it sound like this is something that just happens out of the blue," Ken said. He added, "Shortly after we received the recall notice, we called the adjuster for our insurance company, Allstate. We thought GM should be notified to look into whether the recall had something to do with Brooke's crash. The adjuster said he would contact GM. However, we did not hear back from him for months."

Beth interjected, "In the meantime, we began receiving letters from the attorney for the people who were in the car that hit Brooke's car. They had been injured and the attorney wanted information from us about the Cobalt. It was very stressful, and frankly, I was hoping we could be left alone with our grief. Ken, however, was determined to figure out why this had happened. He spent a lot of time on the internet researching Cobalts and learned there were lots of complaints, including the power steering complaints. Although I understood why Ken was doing what he was doing, I did not believe it would lead to anything. We were both dealing with our grief in our own way."

Ken said, "Just last week we got a call from the insurance adjuster saying that he was scheduling an inspection. After his call, we didn't know what to do. Beth and I talked and weren't sure whether we needed to be at the inspection. We assumed we did. So I called the adjuster back and he said we should probably talk to a lawyer about what to do. I told him I don't know any lawyers, and that is when he told us to call Lance Cooper. The adjuster apparently just lost a case against you and said you might be able to help us."

"The inspection of Brooke's Cobalt that Allstate has requested," Ken continued with a tone that told me he'd been waiting to talk to someone about this, "what are they looking for?"

I explained how at this stage the insurance company does a visual inspection as part of their due diligence, to see if anything in the car might have contributed to the accident beyond what is already noted in the police report. After looking over the report, I doubted there was anything more than met the eye. In my experience, police investigating fatal accidents try to leave no stone unturned. Usually their conclusions are spot-on. Thus far, I had no reason to expect anything different.

"You mean like a manufacturing defect?" Ken asked.

"That's part of it," I said. "Really they're just looking for anything beyond driver error that could have caused Brooke to lose control of her car. Since the people in the car who hit Brooke were injured, they probably want Allstate to pay their claims. If Allstate can find someone other than Brooke to blame, they could refuse to pay. The people doing the inspection will not dismantle anything. This is strictly a visual inspection. Normally, the manufacturer, which in this case is General Motors, will need to have someone there as well. If your insurance company hasn't contacted them, I can do that."

I continued, "If you would like, I can make sure your interests are protected by having someone attend the inspection on your behalf." I made this offer even though I normally only represent individuals and families who have been harmed by defective products. Considering what Ken and Beth had already been through, I thought I could at least help them with the vehicle inspection process and make sure Allstate protected them.

I knew King and Spalding, a global law firm with a local Atlanta office, represented General Motors within the state of Georgia and would want to be at this inspection. I had a good relationship with Harold Franklin, a partner who handled GM cases. This wasn't my first case involving GM. Harold and I had squared off several times. The two of us had a good professional relationship. While we didn't have the kind of relationship where we'd go to a Braves game together, I knew Harold a bit more personally than any other defense lawyer, having seen him at prayer breakfasts in the past. Calling Harold to alert him to any inspection of Brooke's car was more than a professional courtesy, however. If inspectors did happen to find something, we needed someone representing GM on-site to verify we had not tampered with possible evidence in case of a lawsuit. I did not anticipate this case going that far.

While my offer seemed to set Beth at ease, Ken clearly had more on his mind.

"Is there anything else"? I asked.

"Yes," Ken said. "Brooke's car had been in a repair shop the day before the accident. She took it in because it stalled while she was driving through a neighborhood. The engine just quit running, although it started right back up. I told her she needed to take it in to the shop right away. The next day I even followed her to the shop where she had most of her work done, Thornton Chevrolet, just in case her car died on her again."

"What did they do to her car to fix it?" I asked.

Ken explained how the dealership cleaned the fuel injectors and replaced the fuel filter. Thornton also recommended the shifter assembly be replaced because GM had issued a service bulletin concerning the shifter. Service bulletins are issued for performance issues rather than safety problems. "It was going to cost her another $350, so I told her she should get a second opinion before she spent that kind of money, since she'd never had any problems with the shifter before," Ken said. "When she picked up the car, they assured her that they had fixed the stalling problem."

He paused. "The day after she picked the car up from the dealership, she, uh—" Ken could hardly get the words out. "She lost control of it and died." He dropped his head and appeared to be fighting back tears.

Grief is hard enough to survive. Wondering if you gave your child advice which may have had tragic consequences might make it impossible to bear.

"I just want to know what really happened," Ken said. There was a tremor in his voice.

While I sympathized with Ken, it was hard to dismiss the official explanation that this was a tragic case of driver error. At this point, I had committed only to help walk them through the vehicle inspection process and make sure Allstate protected their interests. However, if I started digging into the recall notice and the work done on Brooke's car right before her accident, I'd soon be pulled into doing much more. I wasn't sure I wanted to do that.

The timing of the Melton case wasn't ideal for me from professional and personal standpoints. After an eight- or nine-year run of successful results in cases, I lost three very large cases between 2006 and 2009. Because I represent people bringing a lawsuit involving faulty products, I do not receive a fee unless I win the case. Our firm also covers all of the cost of investigating, filing, and seeing through to completion every case I take. On average, those costs run into the hundreds of thousands of dollars, sometimes as high as half a million for some cases. The three cases I lost in a row were all expensive cases. I went more than a year without getting paid, and my firm ended up close to two million dollars in debt. My wife had to make arrangements with our mortgage company to keep us in our house. On top of that, all three cases involved automobile manufacturers. In the year immediately before the Meltons' visit, our firm had managed to turn things around and get back on reasonably solid financial footing. The memory of three consecutive losses made me much more cautious about the cases I took on.

Also, I found that circumstances at home demanded more of my time and energy. During my children's growing-up years, I tried to strike the right balance between work and home, but of late I found the demands of fatherhood made it hard to concentrate on anything else. I still gave my clients my all, but my fire for work did not burn as bright as it once did. Sleepless nights as a dad to five teenage and young adult children will do this for any father.

Even with so many reasons not to take on Ken and Beth as clients, something told me to listen to them. Call it a gut feeling, call it intuition based on twenty years of experience, but I believe it was providence. In spite of all the very good reasons why I should not become more involved, I ended our appointment by saying, "Let me look into this and see if there might be some way I can help."

As I walked Ken and Beth out of my office, I had no idea I had just signed up for the most important case of my career. At this stage, I didn't even know whether the car had a defect. I had a power steering recall and the suspicious timing of her getting her car back from the shop the day before she lost control of it. That wasn't much to go on, and in product liability cases, the burden of proof is on the plaintiff to show negligence which resulted in harm. The laws in the state of Georgia also guard against frivolous lawsuits. That means I couldn't file a suit against GM just to go on a fishing expedition hoping to find something wrong. Someone losing control of their car on a rainy night was not sufficient grounds for a case. There had to be more. The only way to find out if there was more was to start digging.

CHAPTER 2

An Inevitable Decision

Agreeing to help the Meltons was not, on the face of it, a sound business decision, but I did not go into law to become a businessman. In fact, my distaste for the corporate world drove my decision to go to law school in the first place.

A counselor at the University of California, Berkeley suggested law school to me shortly before I graduated with a major in political science/economics. Looking back, I see how my choice of majors made law school seem like the obvious choice, but it wasn't to me. I wasn't sure what I wanted to do with my degree. Only after my friends began accepting positions in investment banking and other corporate type work did I realize that none of that was for me. Not sure what to do, I met with a placement counselor and that set the course of my life.

The fact that I even graduated from college was anything but a sure thing four years earlier. During my high school years in Southern California, I envisioned myself playing professional football someday. Football was pretty much my life back then. I was a running back on our high school team, which won a state championship. College scouts came to some of our games. Two Division I colleges even offered me a scholarship, Kansas and Hawaii. Given the choice of spending four years surrounded by wheat fields or palm trees, I obviously chose the latter, no offense to Kansas. To me it felt like a match made in heaven.

I'd get to play football, go to school for free, and live in paradise. If everything went according to my eighteen-year-old self's plans, I'd do so well that an NFL team would come calling after I graduated, if not before.

My life plans all fell apart the morning I was set to sign my national letter of intent to go to Hawaii. The coach who had recruited me called and told me that another running back they'd been pursuing had surprised them by agreeing to come there. Because they had a limited number of scholarships to hand out, signing him meant they had to rescind my scholarship offer. I told the coach I understood and everything would be okay, but inside I was crushed. I'd already closed the door on Kansas as well as some smaller schools that had also recruited me. They all moved on to other players. That left me on the outside looking in. To make matters worse, my parents' relationship wasn't in the best place and they ended up divorcing. All of this together left me adrift. Instead of preparing myself for upcoming football practices, I took a job cleaning pools right after my high school graduation. At the time I thought that's what I was going to do for the rest of my life.

Eventually I pulled myself together enough to enroll in a local junior college where I went out for the football team. That didn't last. I drifted a little longer, then went to another school, dropped out, and repeated the process until I eventually finished my first two years of school at Santa Ana Junior College, where I did fairly well on the football team. Unfortunately, I suffered an injury during the middle of my second season which caused most colleges to lose interest in recruiting me. The coaches at UC Berkeley, however, told me that while they could not offer me a scholarship, they could offer me a preferred walk-on admission. Both my mom and dad went to UC Berkeley, so I was familiar with the university. I jumped on their offer since, without football, I'd never get in. I was a decent enough student, but my grades alone were not good enough to be admitted into a university this selective. After making the football team as a walk-on, I played only one year. By now even I realized professional football was not in my future. That's when I got more serious about school, which ultimately led to the conversation with the placement counselor not long before I graduated.

Finding God's Plan

When I started my college journey, I wasn't just adrift in terms of what I wanted to do with my life. I was also adrift spiritually. While I was growing up, my family attended church sporadically, but we went enough to give me a basic foundation in the things of God. In junior high and high school, I often went to various church camps and youth programs with my friends. Eventually I went to an Assembly of God youth group after one of my friends invited me to go with him. Every summer that church took a group of high school students to a camp up at Hume Lake in the Sierra Nevada mountains. During the summer after my junior year, I heard someone share how Jesus gave his life for us on the cross. It wasn't like it was my first time to hear this, but for some reason the message hit home that night. I prayed and had a conversion experience while sitting around a campfire under the Sierra Nevada night sky.

My life changed after that, but only for a time. After the dual blows of losing my scholarship to Hawaii and my parents' marriage falling apart, I sort of wandered away from God. I still believed, and if someone asked me about religion, I'd tell them I was a Christian, but my life didn't exactly show it, especially while I was bouncing around between junior colleges. However, when I started at UC Berkeley, one of my fraternity brothers invited me to attend a Campus Crusade for Christ meeting. I kept going all through my time there. It felt good to reconnect somewhat with God, although I was still prone to wander.

And then I met a girl, *the* girl, it turned out, although I didn't know it at the time. I wasn't even looking for any kind of long-term relationship, which was good because it took a long time for the first meeting to turn into a relationship. This girl lived in Georgia and I lived in Southern California. That we even met counts as an act of God.

After my first year of college, I went out to Marietta, Georgia, to work construction with my uncle and younger cousin. While I was growing up, my grandmother lived out there and so did my aunt, which meant we made quite a few trips back there. After my parents split up, I needed some stability family-wise, and my uncle Howard and aunt Carole provided it. When my uncle Howard offered me the job, I jumped on it. I had no idea what I wanted to do with my life, so giving construction a shot for a summer sounded great. For a kid from Orange County, California, where the temperature is nearly the same year-round, working outside in the Georgia summer heat and humidity worked out about like you'd expect. By the end of the summer I still didn't know what I wanted to do with my life, but I knew what I didn't want to do.

The best thing to come out of that summer of 1982 came when my aunt Carole set me up on a blind date with the daughter of one of her friends. That first date with Sonja didn't exactly scream long-term future. She asked me a lot of questions about my faith and my relationship with God. My answers were ambivalent, to say the least. Ambivalence toward God did not rank high on Sonja's list of qualities she looked for in a man. There was not a second date that summer, and we didn't see each other again for another two years.

The next summer my aunt and uncle recommended me for a job as a summer clerk with a local Marietta lawyer. I had no inclination of becoming a lawyer, not yet at least. I took the job because I'd get to spend the summer with my Georgia family, and I could work indoors. I did not see Sonja that summer. As it turned out, she spent that summer doing mission work in what was then called Upper Volta, but is today Burkina Faso. My job as a law clerk had been her job. I was basically her replacement for that year.

The next summer I went back to the same law office, and to my pleasant surprise, Sonja was there for the summer as well. I asked her out again and, to my great relief, she agreed to see me again. We dated through that summer and continued our relationship, albeit long distance, after I returned to school at UC Berkeley. Conversations about God remained a regular part of our time together. Most of our conversations were through letters since cell phones did not exist, and I could not afford to pay for long-distance phone calls. Between talking with Sonja and going to Campus Crusade for Christ, I found myself moving back toward God, rekindling the relationship which began next to a campfire at Hume Lake so many years before.

I graduated from UC Berkeley in December 1985 and moved to Marietta to work as a clerk in the same law firm where I'd worked during the summer. Being geographically closer to Sonja was the real reason I worked there. Sonja was finishing her last year of law school at Mercer University in Macon, about a two-hour drive from Marietta. I also started applying to law schools. I applied and was accepted to Emory University School of Law in Atlanta and was all set to enroll there in the fall of 1986. But then I panicked. I knew I was falling in love with Sonja, but after living through my parents' divorce, I was afraid I didn't have what it takes to commit to a relationship that might end in marriage. Rather than enroll at Emory, I ran away to go to law school in Boston. I justified it by saying I wanted to experience another part of the country. Sonja didn't buy it. From her perspective, that pretty much put an end to any thought of a future together. She moved on and started dating other people.

I, however, did not.

I really enjoyed Boston at first. A new city. A new experience. I remember landing at Logan Airport with my life's possessions in a couple of duffel bags. I took public transportation, the "T," to the Boston University School of Law. I then walked to the housing office, and the staff person directed me to a bulletin board which had potential places to live. I noticed an index card with a Marlborough Street address. It was within a mile of the campus. So I began walking. I soon found myself in the Back Bay of Boston, just off the Charles River. It was a beautiful neighborhood, unlike anything I had ever seen growing up in Southern California.

I knocked on the door of the three-story brownstone home, and Larry opened the door, welcomed me into his home, and then showed me where I would be living if I chose to. It was the "crow's nest" at the top of the house, consisting of one room and a tiny bathroom. It was a perfect place for me because all I expected to do my first year of law school was study, eat, and sleep.

I loved the Back Bay neighborhood and Boston in general. There was a small grocery store on the corner, and I could walk to Fenway Park. The fall of 1986 was when the Boston Red Sox finally made it back to the World Series, and the city was nuts about their Red Sox. Although I didn't have much money, I was able to buy a ticket for a seat in the outfield bleachers for one of the Red Sox games. What an experience. This was also the time of the heated rivalry between Larry Bird's Celtics and Magic Johnson's Lakers. Of course, being from Southern California, I was all in for the Lakers' showtime. Most of my first-year law school friends were Celtics fans, which made rooting for the Lakers that much more fun.

Although I enjoyed Boston, like any first-year law student, most of my time consisted of going to class and studying. I also found myself constantly thinking about Sonja. The more I thought about her, the more I realized I'd made a *huge* mistake moving to Boston instead of going to school in Atlanta. I didn't just miss her. I knew I wanted to spend the rest of my life with her. The question was how to spring this on her. I thought she loved me, at least before I turned down Emory to move to Boston.

Studying became difficult because Sonja was the only thing I could think about. I made up my mind that I was going to ask her to marry me even though I had no idea what her answer would be. I then called my aunt Carole, who along with Sonja's mother set us up on our first blind date, and told her my plans to fly to Marietta and propose to Sonja the next weekend. I could tell Carole was excited, but she had some concerns. Carole told me Sonja would not be in town the next weekend. My aunt didn't have the heart to tell me, but

Sonja had a date with someone else. After waiting a couple of weeks, I flew down to Marietta and gave Sonja a call. She was—how should I put it?—lukewarm at best. I had to talk her into even going out to get a cup of coffee with me. As we were having coffee and engaging in small talk, I nervously brought out a ring, showed it to her, and asked her to marry me. She didn't exactly jump at the opportunity. "Uh, why are you doing this? Why are you popping the question out of the blue?" Sonja later told me her first thought was, "You have just ruined a perfectly good friendship."

Testing me, she then asked, "How many children do you want to have?" I said, "Five." I surprised her with my certainty, not to mention the number. She peppered me with more questions. I sort of prepared myself for her to say no. Finally, she asked, "How long can I take before I give you an answer?"

"I'll be in Boston for a year, so you can take a year if you need it," I said.

Thankfully, Sonja didn't take that long. During my Thanksgiving break, I flew from Boston to Palm Desert, California, to spend time with my father. Before I left, Sonja called and said she would like to spend Thanksgiving with me. She flew to Los Angeles International Airport, where my brother, Scott, picked her up to drive her the two hours down to Palm Desert. Scott was a senior in high school at the time. But the drive took a lot longer than it should have. As Scott and Sonja drove to Palm Desert, Sonja asked him to pull over because she felt sick to her stomach. A short time later, she had him pull over again. And again.

By the time the two of them got to our house in Palm Desert, Sonja was a wreck. I thought she had caught a bug and was going to be sick all weekend. I found out the real reason for her "sickness" a short time after they arrived. She pulled me outside, hugged me, and said, "I've prayed a lot about this, and . . ." She started to cry. "God told me that you are the man I am supposed to marry."

I kissed her and held her tight. "So you aren't sick?" I asked.

"No," she laughed. "I was so nervous it made me sick to my stomach."

The next summer I transferred to Emory. Sonja and I were married before classes began in the summer of 1987. Our first house was a guest house at the base of Kennesaw Mountain National Park. The park was our back yard, which was a wonderful place to start a marriage. Over the next two years, Sonja continued to work as a prosecutor, which helped to pay for my law school. We got involved in a local church as well as Chuck Colson's Prison Fellowship (PF). Colson, the former Nixon hatchet man who came to Christ shortly before going to prison for his part in the Watergate scandal, started Prison Fellowship not long after he was released from federal prison. His books had an impact on Sonja and me and our understanding of what it meant to live out our faith in the real world. For us, getting involved in PF felt like the natural thing to do.

With PF, we had an inmate, Bill Smith, stay in our home for a week as part of a program to help prisoners transition back into civilian life. On the Friday night Bill was with us, we took him water-skiing on Sonja's parents' boat. I'll never forget Bill turning to us and saying, "When the brothers hear I learned how to water-ski in prison, they're never going to believe me."

In 1989, two years after Sonja and I were married, I was about to graduate from Emory. Sonja was pregnant and had already made up her mind that she was going to quit her job and stay home with our baby. I was completely in agreement with her decision. Some people said she wasted her education by practicing law for only three years. Sonja's answer showed the independent spirit I love so much in her. She told the critics, "I loved being a lawyer, but I love being a mom more."

With a new job on the horizon and a baby on the way, Sonja and I were ready to dive into this next phase of our lives together. I had job offers from firms in Atlanta, Dallas, San Francisco, Los Angeles, and Orange County. We talked through them all. Sonja said, "If we're going to move away from Atlanta, I would love to live in Dallas or San Francisco." I, however, really wanted to move back home to Orange

County, which is what we ended up doing. I started my new job with a large firm. A few months after we moved, Rachel was born. Life was pretty much perfect, except . . .

I hated my job. The firm represented large corporate clients, who were either suing, or being sued by, other large corporate clients. Over the course of nine months I spent most of my time sitting in a warehouse type room, going over documents related to cases from which I was far removed. The work felt far from satisfying, as if all I did was compile billable hours for the firm. Nothing about what I did felt like it made any difference for anyone. I went home after work and tried to put on a happy face, but Sonja could see right through it. When she asked what was wrong, I told her that I didn't become a lawyer to become a cog in a corporate machine. During law school I saw how an attorney can make a huge difference in people's lives. I know I was young and idealistic, but that's what I wanted to do as well. As corny as it may sound, I wanted to pursue justice for my clients and help them when they'd been wronged. I could not do that shuffling papers in a warehouse.

About three or four months into my time with the firm, I had an epiphany. One Saturday morning I found myself sitting around a large boardroom table with one of the partners and several of the associates in our firm. The discussion centered around a case involving a real estate company we represented. As the people around me talked about the case, I looked at the partner and thought, *I cannot imagine doing this the rest of my life. They could offer me a partnership, right now today, and I would never take it. I don't belong here.* Not long after, I began looking for an opportunity back in Georgia. Sonja loved the idea of moving back. So did I.

A New Adventure

I received an offer to go to work for a general practice attorney in Marietta named Jean Johnson. Jean did a little of everything from family law to criminal defense to personal injury, whatever his clients needed. Working with him appealed to me because of the proximity to family, but also because it gave me a chance to try different areas of the law while closely interacting with my clients. Less appealing was the 60 percent pay cut I took to move from a multinational corporate law firm to a solo practitioner in Marietta. I took the job anyway.

Working as an associate for Jean set me on the professional path I have traveled for almost thirty years. Jean was, and is, a very well-respected trial lawyer in the community. As a result, he represented many clients in significant personal injury and wrongful death cases. Because he and I were the only trial lawyers in the practice, early on I gained invaluable experience working on substantial cases. Unlike my previous job, within a few months of joining Jean, I was interviewing clients, drafting important pleadings, taking depositions, and doing whatever else was necessary to prepare a case for trial. Jean helped me understand how important it is to make each client feel like he or she is your only client. This was particularly important for our practice since we represented individuals and families in the worst of circumstances.

I wanted to make a difference in my clients' lives, and I had the chance in my very first case I took to trial. A poor, very young couple from west Georgia came to our firm in a case of medical malpractice. After they discovered she was pregnant, they traveled into Atlanta regularly for prenatal care at a free clinic. The same doctor provided care for her throughout her pregnancy. The young mom's due date came and went. At forty-one and a half weeks, she came back into the office for an ultrasound. The test showed the baby was in distress because of oligohydramnios, which meant the mom's amniotic fluid was drying up fast. She should have been sent to the hospital immediately for them to induce labor or do an emergency C-section. Instead she was sent home. A few days later the couple returned to the clinic with the mom saying, "I can't feel my baby moving." Sadly, they lost the baby at full term because the doctor ignored the test results.

Being the young, idealistic lawyer that I was, I thought the case was open and shut. Jean was more cautious. He explained that the jury may sympathize with the doctor who provided free care and overlook or forgive his negligence. I was, in a word, incredulous. How could any jury rule against this young couple when the doctor was clearly at fault? Unfortunately, Jean was prophetic and the jury did just that. The jury felt for the couple, yet they viewed the doctor as a very kind man who volunteered his services at this clinic. Besides, at only eighteen and nineteen years of age, this couple would have more children.

Trying to explain why we lost was the hardest thing I'd ever had to do. "But Mr. Cooper," they said to me, "he didn't send the report." I had to just look at them and say, I know. "And our baby's dead because of that." I know, was all I could say. I had no answers then and I still do not today. I think about this couple every time another set of parents comes to see me due to the loss of a child, and that includes Ken and Beth Melton.

My first product liability case came in 1992 when Jean and I represented a twenty-two-year-old widow who lost her husband when a tire blew out on his Ford Bronco II, which caused the vehicle to roll over, taking the man's life. Her husband did not have life insurance, leaving his young wife to fend for herself with their six-month-old son.

I had no experience with product liability cases, and I needed to learn quickly. In 1992, I couldn't google Bronco II lawsuits, so I began my investigation by calling lawyers I knew who had product liability experience. I soon found a lawyer in Cornelia, a small town in North Georgia, who knew about the Bronco II's rollover history. I called Ed Strain and asked if he wouldn't mind speaking with me about his experience. I hoped he might give me a few minutes on the phone. Instead, a few minutes into the call, he invited me to come to his office and meet with him and his partner, Dennis Cathey, to help me prepare to take on Ford and General Tire. I was dumbfounded. Why would two successful trial lawyers want to take the time to meet with me and share what they learned with no expectation they would receive anything in return? I decided not to ask questions and, instead, gratefully accepted the offer.

The next week I drove to Cornelia, and Ed and Dennis welcomed me into their office. In the back of the office was a huge room piled high with boxes, many of which contained documents produced by Ford relating to the Bronco II. Then Ed began to tell me the story. In a nutshell, in the early 1980s, Ford designed the Bronco II as a small sport utility vehicle to compete with the Jeep CJ, a very popular and profitable SUV. Unfortunately, when Ford began on-road testing of the Bronco II, they discovered it was very unstable. It had the propensity to roll over in accident avoidance maneuvers. Think of a child darting into a road and a Bronco II driver swerving to avoid the child. The Bronco II would likely roll over under those circumstances.

After Ford learned of this rollover problem, its engineers came up with five options to address the problem. The first option was the most expensive solution. The fifth option was the least expensive and least effective. Ford chose the fifth option. As a result, Bronco IIs started rolling over as soon as people started buying them. Injuries and fatalities climbed, thousands of them, all from Ford's poor design and refusal to do anything about it. Ed showed me the Ford documents which supported everything he told me.

I asked how he had obtained these documents. "Ford didn't just hand them over to you willingly, did they?" I asked. Ed responded that he and other lawyers around the country had worked together in their lawsuits against Ford and persuaded courts to order Ford to produce all Bronco II documents. As a result of these efforts, Ford had to produce these damaging documents. Without them, Ford's conduct never would have been uncovered.

It gets worse.

Ed then showed me the testimony of the Ford employees who had prepared these documents. They were devastating for Ford. After reading their testimony, there was no question that Ford put profits over the safety of its customers when it chose not to spend the money to properly fix the Bronco II. That day my eyes were opened. I saw how our civil justice system actually works to give individuals and families the right to hold corporations accountable for their negligence and, in some cases, fraudulent concealment. I also began to understand how important it is to use the law to make sure corporations produce all evidence relevant in a case, especially evidence which may be harmful to them.

Armed with the documents and wisdom I gleaned from Ed and Dennis, Jean and I filed a lawsuit on behalf of our client against Ford and General Tire. Not surprisingly, Ford settled early. General Tire was not so forthcoming. I then took what I learned from Ed and Dennis and began pressuring General Tire to produce documents regarding the design and testing of its tires and any other lawsuits relating to these tires. Not surprisingly, when the court ordered General Tire to produce all documents, we learned that the company not only knew its tires had design defects but also concealed these defects from the federal government. Shortly before trial, General Tire also decided to settle.

The result gave me a great deal of satisfaction. Not only did we secure a good settlement for a young mom that gave her and her son a stable financial future, we also helped uncover some unsettling facts about defective products both companies preferred to keep hidden. Being the one to help uncover these facts and to secure justice for my client did more than make me feel good, like I'd done a good job. I knew I'd found the area of the law upon which I wanted to focus.

Finding my specialty was not enough. In the mid-1990s I took on a case which opened my eyes to the need to take more of a missional approach to my work. The case, like the Meltons', started with a parent's worst nightmare. A set of grieving parents, Melissa and John Lawler, came to me when their twenty-two-year-old son was killed in a car accident. As with the Meltons, he was their oldest child. They, too, had a younger daughter. They were devastated by the loss. Our meetings together involved lots of tears as they lived out their grief.

Yet this couple remained hopeful because of their faith in Christ. In our first meeting they even asked me if I was a believer. To them, it was crucial that their attorney share their faith.

Over the next two years I came to share much more with them. I attended a memorial service at their church for their son. I also watched as they worked through their grief by helping others. They took a particular interest in my children. Even years after their case was settled, Melissa continued to bring gifts to my five children at Christmas.

The Lawlers' example challenged me to be more intentional in the way in which I express my faith through my work. Most of the people who walk through my door come carrying a huge load of pain. They've suffered a life-altering loss either through personal injury or the loss of a loved one. While working to help restore their lives to something close to what they had before is important, it is not enough. Second Corinthians 1:3–4 tells us that God comforts us so that we might comfort others as they walk through the pain life can deal out. Over the past twenty years, I've worked to do just that. I don't just want to help my clients' legal needs. I and my staff also work to help with their emotional and spiritual needs. That doesn't mean we try to force God on anyone. Rather, we simply make this available for those receptive to it. Honestly, it has changed the way I view my work and its purpose.

This sense of calling to help clients get through nightmare situations is what compelled me to take the first steps in the Melton case. Yet because I view my work as an extension of living out God's purpose for my life, I can say the same thing about every case I consider.

CHAPTER 3

More Questions
Than Answers

I wish I could say I dove into the Melton case with unbridled
enthusiasm. After all, my work is my mission, and making a difference
in people's lives is my goal. Here were two people who clearly needed
my help. How could I not plunge in full force? Perhaps I would have
twenty years earlier. Now I found myself not necessarily hesitant, but
perhaps tepid. In Luke 14:28, Jesus asked, "Suppose one of you wants
to build a tower. Won't you first sit down and estimate the cost?"
When I was young and idealistic, sure, I could change the world. I
rarely gave the cost a thought. My idealism evolved into hubris when
I experienced nearly a decade-long run of success, a run I assumed
would continue on unchecked. It did not. As I mentioned in the first
chapter, I lost three major cases between 2006 and 2009, which left
my firm nearly $2 million in debt and my family's financial future in
doubt. While both my firm and my family managed to get our heads
above water over the next couple of years, I remained hesitant to take
on a costly and risky case.

But it wasn't just the losses and resulting debt that gave me pause.
One must play a certain game when entering the legal system, a game
filled with motions and countermotions and delay tactics. As the

counsel for the plaintiff, I carry the burden of proof. The other side knows this. They also know much of the proof I need can be found in their paper trails of documents they do their best never to reveal in spite of the motions I file to force them to do just that. They ask for delays, then produce a fraction of what I want hidden within an avalanche of documents I do not need. The game is expensive, time consuming, and exhausting. Increasingly, whenever I think about plunging into another round, I have to ask myself if I am up to it, because once I step into the ring, I will not step out until I've won or lost.

Thankfully, not long before Ken and Beth's initial appointment, I had a case that helped kick-start my zeal for what I do. A young mom was driving home from work in an SUV on a freeway in Atlanta when another SUV next to her suddenly went out of control and veered right into her. The collision caused her SUV to flip over while traveling 60 mph. She struck her head while being thrown around violently in her car before it finally came to a stop. The resulting traumatic brain injury left her in the hospital for months and in a rehabilitation facility for even longer. After she returned home, she still needed attendants to care for her and her two-year-old son.

Unfortunately, the driver of the SUV that hit her had minimum insurance limits. The driver, however, said she lost control because her rear tire failed. We then obtained the tire, which was made by Michelin, and had an engineer inspect it. Just as the driver claimed, the engineer determined a defect had caused the tread to separate, resulting in the loss of control in the collision.

Michelin was probably the most respected tire company in the world. Confident that we could prove the tire defect caused the crash and our client's severe injuries, we chose to file a lawsuit against Michelin. Not surprisingly, Michelin refused to accept responsibility and blamed, among others, our client for causing her injuries. I then did what I had learned almost twenty years before in my first product liability case: I began digging for answers about what Michelin knew and when it knew it about this defective tire. After a protracted battle, Michelin finally produced documents showing it knew about dozens of other failures of this tire model, which caused numerous deaths and severe injuries. Once forced to disclose this damning evidence, Michelin chose to settle with our client rather than face a jury.

I could not stop smiling the day I delivered the news to my client that we secured a settlement which would provide for the future financial needs of her and her son. More than winning, the case rejuvenated me. The case reaffirmed my faith in the civil justice system.

After decades in the trenches, I find it is easy to get jaded. I sometimes lose sight of the fact that the threat of a civil action is far more effective than government oversight in compelling businesses to do the right thing and holding them accountable when they do not.

This Michelin tire case reminded me why I do what I do. I needed it.

Let the Games Begin

The civil justice system process often moves at a glacial pace. Each case plods along, one legal step and maneuver at a time. The Melton case was no different. I kicked the whole thing off with a short phone call to Harold Franklin, the chief attorney locally for all things GM at Atlanta's King and Spalding law firm.

Harold was quite pleasant when I called, which was what I expected. The two of us had faced off in many cases, but always had a very cordial relationship. While I cannot remember the exact words of our conversation, basically I said something like, "I have a couple whose daughter was involved in an accident involving a GM product. The officer on the scene ruled driver error. The other car involved in the crash is considering filing suit against the insurance company, and my clients may well be named in the suit. As part of their due diligence in this matter, the insurance company wants to do a visual inspection of the car for any possible defects. My office will be there for my clients. I thought you would probably want someone there as well since your firm represents General Motors."

Harold said something along the lines of, "I appreciate that, Lance. So it's just a visual inspection? They don't plan on taking anything apart, do they?"

"Correct. A visual inspection only. We'll also want to download the crash data from the SDM (Supplemental Restraint System Diagnostic Module)." The SDM functions as a car's "black box." It digitally records five seconds of precrash and crash data, including vehicle speed, engine RPM, braking, etc. The data also tells you about the forces in the crash, such as vehicle speed at the moment of impact.

"That shouldn't be a problem," Harold said. "I'll get someone from ESIS out there for it." ESIS is a third-party claims administrator for GM.

"Okay, great," I said. "My office will set up a time and we'll go from there."

"Sounds great. By the way, what kind of car is it?" Harold asked.

"A 2005 Cobalt," I said.

"Okay, thanks," Harold said. He ended up sending a man named Ryan Jahr to do the inspection.

After calling Harold Franklin, I then called Dave Paul at Applied Technical Services, or ATS, to line up someone to inspect Highway 92 where the accident took place and to request Jeff Hyatt for the vehicle inspection. I needed the road inspection to evaluate the possibility that standing water caused the accident. As for Jeff, he worked with me on a case involving a Chrysler vehicle that dropped from park to neutral without warning, causing the car to roll down an incline and hurt someone. While the Melton case was a little different in that we needed to know if the power steering had caused a problem, I felt confident Jeff would be able to help me get to the bottom of this.

Doreen Lundrigan, my primary paralegal since 2001 and an indispensable member of my team, then contacted Brooke's insurance company, Allstate, and made arrangements with the wrecker yard for the inspection. Allstate still had Brooke's car, which is normal protocol with an outstanding claim. After working around everyone's schedule, we set March 22 for the actual inspection date. Doreen agreed to go for me. At this time the Melton case still carried the "I'll see what I can do" status. I had other cases which demanded more of my time. Besides, I knew I could not add anything to the team already assembled. Even though I've worked on over a hundred automotive cases, I'm not exactly the most mechanical or technical guy in the world.

Inspection

A couple of weeks after my initial round of phone calls, Dave from ATS called me. "I sent someone out to Highway 92 during a rainstorm," he said.

"And?" I asked.

"The road drains properly. We found no standing water or anything else that might indicate improper road maintenance contributed to the accident," he said.

"So you can definitively rule out the possibility that she hit a pool of water which then caused her to lose control of the car?" I asked.

"Yes. Absolutely," Dave replied.

I thanked him, and while the news was hardly devastating, I was a little disappointed. Standing water due to poor road design could have wrapped this all up very simply. Now we had to keep digging, if there was even anything to dig for.

That brought us back to Brooke's car. When Doreen returned from the visual inspection at the salvage yard, I called her into my office to ask how it went.

"You know, your basic visual inspection," she replied. "Not a lot you can tell from just looking when you can't even start the car."

"Anything stand out?" I asked.

"Just the obvious. Right side of the car sustained most of the damage, which is consistent with the police report. That's about it. Hard to tell much of anything else. However, the steering wheel seemed to be locked up. Could be something."

"Interesting," I said. "Maybe Jeff will be able to tell us more."

I set up a meeting with Jeff Hyatt on April 12 at ATS. That gave him time to go over the data he retrieved from the car's crash data recorder. Unfortunately, he didn't find much more than Doreen had already told me. "I did a thorough vehicle inspection, but I didn't find anything inconsistent with the conclusions of the police report," Jeff told me.

"What about the steering wheel?" I asked. "Doreen told me it was in the lock position."

"It was, but it is impossible to know whether that had something to do with the accident or if the severity of the impact of the accident caused the wheel to lock up. The only way to know for sure is to disassemble it. But that's not really my area of expertise," Jeff said.

"And I doubt GM will let us do that," I said. "What about the data from the SDM?"

"Honestly, I don't see anything from my perspective that could explain her losing control of the vehicle. But that data was hard to understand. Some of it just didn't make sense."

"How so?" I asked.

"The SDM data printout had to be off. At five seconds before the crash, she was going 58. At four seconds she was going 57. Then at three seconds and two and one, it showed her speed as zero. Same with the RPMs. Her engine speed dropped to zero before the accident like the engine had been turned off. There has to be some sort of problem with the data recorder because a car doesn't go from 57 to zero in less than a second. That just can't happen," Jeff said.

"What do you think the problem might be?" I asked.

"I have no idea. But that's not the strangest data. According to this, the car had switched from 'run' to 'accessory' position."

"Which means what?" I asked.

"Run is what it says. That's the position the key is in after you start your car. Accessory is the position where the engine shuts off, but some of the electrical systems like the radio still work. Basically, it's what you do when you park the car while waiting for someone, but you still want to listen to the radio. The key should never be in the accessory position when the car is moving," Jeff explained.

"Why would it be in accessory?" I asked.

"That I cannot tell you," Jeff said. "I am not an expert in this download area. I think you're going to need to find someone who specializes in this to help you understand what, if anything, the information on this report means."

"Did you find anything else?" I asked.

"She had an aftermarket security system. The GM guys made sure I noticed that," he said. "Overall, I'd say there's nothing definitive yet to go on here."

Allstate reached the same conclusion. Not long after the vehicle inspection, they reached an agreement with the driver and passenger of the other car. No lawsuit was ever filed by the occupants of the other car. Ken and Beth Melton did not need me to protect their interests any longer.

That should have been the end of the story. A young woman died in a tragic accident on a rainy night on her birthday. The police concluded it was driver error. "Driving too fast for conditions," was how they put it. Nothing that came up in the visual inspection screamed that the police report was wrong.

But . . .

I had a feeling there might be something there. I kept coming back to the locked steering wheel. Yes, the force of the impact might have caused it to lock in place, but it was not a frontal impact. The other car slammed into the right rear quarter panel, with most of the impact concentrated directly on the back wheel. How could that cause the steering wheel to lock in place? While it was far from a smoking gun, I could not in good conscience just walk away without at least taking the electronic power steering system apart to see if there was some sort of problem. Ken had been adamant that their daughter was too good of a driver to just lose control of her car. "Something had to have happened," he insisted. I'd come this far. I did not see the harm in sticking with this a little while longer to see where it might lead.

Unfortunately, going forward meant convincing GM to let us take the steering assembly apart. Like any corporation in the world, they do not normally agree to extensive vehicle inspections unless they are compelled to by something more than a phone call. I knew better than to even try. Even so, I had a couple of conversations with Harold Franklin about the inspection. "Jeff from ATS told me the steering wheel is locked up and the only way to know for certain what caused it is to disassemble it," I said.

Harold's reply did not surprise me. "Lance, you know we can't just allow you to do that, not without proper protocols in place." Proper protocols meant after a lawsuit had been filed. He went on to tell me why there were no grounds for a suit. He also questioned why I was even bothering with this Melton thing since it was a tragic case of a young woman losing control of her car from driving too fast in the rain. Clearly, I needed to look elsewhere for answers.

I had one other person to try. Chris Caruso was known as the automobile airbag expert in our area. A car's crash data recorder is part of the airbag system, recording information on when and why an airbag deploys. That made Chris the obvious choice to try to make some sense of the SDM data. He had worked at Delphi, which was the company that made many of the electrical components, including the airbag system and ignition switch in the Cobalt. He later worked for General Motors for a while before going into business on his own in the early 2000s as a consultant. I sent him the data hoping he could help me out.

A Curious Coincidence

Ken and Beth came back to my office in May to talk about the inspection and where we should go from here. Three months had already gone by since our first appointment. To be honest, we were no closer to answers as to why Brooke lost control of her car than we were in February. Because GM raised a question about the aftermarket security system on Brooke's car, I had Ken bring in the key fob that controlled it. He also brought something else he'd found when sorting through Brooke's things. "Our daughter kept notes about whatever was going on from day to day, little notes to remind her of whatever she needed to do or things she needed to fix. That's where we found this," Ken said.

He handed me a page pulled out of a small spiral notebook. At the top of the page were the words "Fuel pump?"

"These were the notes she took with her when she took her car into the shop a few days before the accident," Ken said.

Her bullet-pointed list read:

- Key locking in the ignition
- Suddenly shutting off while driving and unable to turn vehicle
- Interior paint rubbing off numbers on radio panel
- Metallic covering over interior door handle coming off
- Strange knocking sound while stopped. Sounds like it is coming from the trunk.

Below the list she'd underlined the words "ignition problems."

"Do you know when she wrote all this down?" I asked.

"Right before she took it in to Thornton Chevrolet after her engine cut out on her, I believe," Ken said.

Her second bullet point jumped out at me: "Suddenly shutting off while driving and unable to turn vehicle." We had a locked-up steering wheel. Was there a connection? I wondered. Brooke's writing all this down spoke volumes to me. The problems with her car worried her. I knew a jury would reach the same conclusion, as though Brooke was speaking directly to them even though she was gone.

After talking about the note, we had to make a decision. "Allstate reached a settlement with the people in the other car. They are not going to sue," I explained. "So what we have to decide is where we go from here, if anywhere. You are not going to be sued. Now the question is, are there grounds for you to file suit against GM or against Thornton Chevrolet, and if so, is that something you'd even want to do?"

"What do you mean 'grounds to sue'?" Beth asked. "Did you find something wrong with the car?"

"I do not know yet," I said. "The inspection showed the steering wheel is in the locked position . . ."

"Why would it be locked?" Ken asked.

"I don't know. The only way to know is to disassemble it, and GM will not let us do that unless a suit has been filed," I said. "The data from the crash data recorder, the black box which records the five seconds immediately before an accident, is also puzzling. My inspector didn't know what to make of it."

"What did it show?" Beth asked.

"It recorded the speed of Brooke's car dropping from fifty-something to zero all at once. I have not yet been able to find the answer as to why or even if that has anything at all to do with Brooke's accident," I said.

I paused for a moment while Ken and Beth took all of this in.

"So what we need to decide is whether you want me to keep digging, understanding that this will most likely mean filing suit against General Motors. Or do you want me to stop now?"

Ken and Beth looked at one another before Ken answered for the two of them. "Whatever you think best, Lance. We will follow your lead."

Now it was my turn to make a decision. Given all the uncertainties and how very little I had to go on, winning a suit against GM at this point appeared highly unlikely. But in my years of practice, I'd learned that you never see the answers at the beginning. Immediately after filing a suit, you enter into what is called the discovery process, and I've found there is always lots to discover. I had also grown since my early, idealistic days. I used to charge forward. Now I'd learned that cases like this are usually won by moving ahead slow and steady, being careful not to get ahead of myself or the evidence.

Finally, I answered. "There may not be anything here, but there are at least enough unanswered questions that I think we'd be wise to keep going forward."

"Then that's what we'll do," Ken answered for the both of them.

A few days later, I talked to Chris about what he'd found in the SDM data. Unfortunately, the data left him baffled as well. "The readings are very unusual. I haven't seen anything like this before. I am not going to be able to tell you why this happened, but given my experience with General Motors, I can tell you, they should know why this happened."

I knew if GM had answers, there was only one way I could get them to tell me.

CHAPTER 4

And So It Begins

Three months after Ken and Beth's first appointment, I still had three questions I could not answer. First, did the electronic power steering fail at the time of the wreck, causing Brooke to lose control of her car? If it did, then this problem had to be related to the power steering recall GM issued on March 2, 2010, or four days before she took her car in for service. Ken believed the recall came up when Brooke took her car in for the stalling problem, but Thornton Chevrolet told her they didn't yet have the parts to fix it. The recall also included a delivery stop. A delivery stop simply means a dealership cannot sell a car under recall without first performing the recall repairs. However, nothing in the delivery stop prevented Thornton Chevrolet from sending Brooke on her way without first repairing the power steering when she brought her car in for unrelated repairs.

Whether or not the power steering went out, for some reason the steering locked up either before, during, or as a result of her accident. Why? What made the steering wheel lock up? More important, is that what caused Brooke to lose control of her car? If it was, then did a defect in the car cause the wheel to lock up as it did?

My experts told me the only way to know for sure what had happened with the steering was to take the entire steering assembly apart. I brought that up in a phone call with Harold Franklin, hoping to get permission to do that without having to file a lawsuit first. His response was what I expected. "Lance," he said, "there's really nothing here. The inspection didn't find any problems with the vehicle. The download data doesn't show there was a problem with the vehicle. I think this was just a case where Brooke Melton, for whatever reason, lost control of her car. I don't see how GM could be responsible for that."

I pressed my case anyway. "We could clear all this up pretty easily if we just took the steering system apart. My guys tell me that would tell us definitively one way or another if the power steering was the problem," I said.

Harold did not say no. Instead he said, "Well, I'll talk it over with GM and get back with you."

A month later I still hadn't heard anything, nor did I expect to. Like I wrote in the last chapter, large companies, and even small ones for that matter, don't usually voluntarily do anything that might open them up to being held responsible for an accident, especially one resulting in a death.

Now it was decision time for me. Did I feel strongly enough about the locked steering wheel to go ahead and file a lawsuit? I could not answer that. Yet I found myself going back time and again to the notes Brooke kept about the problems with her car prior to taking it in to Thornton Chevrolet. "Suddenly shutting off and unable to turn vehicle," she wrote. Suddenly. I kept turning that over and over in my head. Apparently, she'd researched the problem because she had written "fuel pump" at the top of the page and "ignition problems" on the bottom. Thornton claimed they'd fixed the problem by cleaning her fuel injectors and fuel filter. I'm no mechanic, but those don't seem like the kinds of things that cause a car to suddenly shut off. From what I'd heard, dirty fuel injectors and a clogged fuel filter cause a car to sputter and die. I wondered if her car had died again and if that somehow caused her accident.

Okay. Let's do this, I told myself when I decided to go ahead and file a lawsuit. GM wasn't going to let me take anything apart any other way, and from what I'd been told, this was the only way I could get the answers I was looking for. I also had questions for the people at GM who'd designed the steering system. Once I filed, I could subpoena them along with any pertinent documents which could give me the full story behind the steering recall. In the end, this whole thing could still turn out to be nothing more than a tragic case of driver error. If that's where the evidence took me, so be it. I'd be out whatever money I invested in pursuing the case, but at least I'd have real answers to the questions gnawing at me. Deep down, something told me I wasn't going to be out any money. GM was hiding something. I planned to find out what.

I also included Thornton Chevrolet in the lawsuit. The potential electronic power steering system defect would be General Motors' responsibility. We also believed that Thornton knew about the recall when Brooke took her car in for the stalling problem, even if Brooke had not yet received the recall notice. While the delivery stop in the recall notice did not technically mean they could not release her car to her without first repairing the steering problem, it seemed to me it should have. If a customer buying a brand-new Cobalt could not drive it off the lot without having the recall problem repaired, why did they allow Brooke to drive away in her five-year-old car?

The bigger question with Thornton revolved around the stall problem. They claimed to have fixed it. The next day Brooke lost control of her car and died. Was this more than a coincidence? The SDM data perplexed my experts, but it indicated a loss of power. The data showed the engine's RPM dropped to zero three seconds before the accident. RPMs drop to zero when an engine stalls or dies or is turned off. Why the car lost power was yet to be determined, but it seemed to me that the fact that it had must have meant it contributed to the accident.

I filed the lawsuit on June 24, 2011, in Cobb County, Georgia. Including Thornton Chevrolet in the suit allowed us to file in Georgia state court rather than forcing us into federal court where one must go when the case involves residents of one state suing a business operating in another. The rules are different in state courts than in federal. Georgia law includes a very broad discovery rule, which essentially says if anything is potentially relevant to your case, you must produce it when requested by the other side. This goes for both sides, plaintiffs and defendants. Our suit also landed in front of a no-nonsense judge, Judge Kathryn Tanksley. In my experience, she was very aggressive about making sure both sides comply with their discovery obligations. She did not stand for legal gamesmanship, a fact that made a huge difference as the case played out in front of her.

In terms of the suit itself, we did not name a specific damage amount. In fact, the Meltons and I never discussed money in connection with this suit for nearly two years. For them, this suit was never about money. It was about finding answers to what happened to their daughter on Highway 92 on the night of her twenty-ninth birthday. That search began with the interrogatories (the legal term for questions) that I filed with the suit. I asked a variety of questions, including: Who designed the Cobalt? Who designed the electronic power steering system? Are there other incidents where the power steering caused crashes? We could then subpoena these people for depositions. We also requested all pertinent documents related to the Cobalt electronic power assisted steering recall.

Harold Franklin and I talked a short time after I filed the lawsuit. As I wrote earlier, the two of us had a good relationship, the kind where we could be straight with one another. When Harold first learned I'd filed, he said something like, "Where are you going with this one, Lance? You know, this one doesn't make a lot of sense. The police report is pretty clear about what happened. I don't know how you can possibly think GM was at fault."

"We'll see," I said. "There's a lot about the accident that doesn't fit the police report."

He then said something along the lines of, "You're fishing for something that's not there." I did not learn until much later that Harold was involved in two other cases involving GM cars that bore a striking similarity to ours. How close they were to one another wasn't even clear to Harold or anyone else at that time. If it had been, he most likely would have advised his client to settle our case quickly, and we may well have agreed. Once again, I see the fact that GM initially did not take this lawsuit seriously as providential as well.

Immediately after filing the suit, I bought Brooke's Cobalt from Allstate for the salvage value, somewhere around $500, and had it stored at ATS. Since Allstate had settled all claims related to Brooke's accident, they didn't need it any longer. If I hadn't bought it when I did, it would have ended up crushed in some salvage yard. If that had happened, our case would have been over before it started. There's a simple rule in product liability cases: No product, no case.

Deny, Deny, Deny

GM had thirty days in which to respond to the lawsuit and provide our requested documents in the interrogatories. The lawsuit response came right on time. Over the course of fifteen pages, they offered twenty-two defenses, all of which basically came down to three points: We didn't do anything; the Cobalt is a fine car; and if there is a problem, it's not our fault. They also threw in a few "this suit violates our constitutional rights" for good measure.

I did not expect GM to admit to anything, but their denials reached absurd levels. In paragraph 6 of our complaint, I wrote, "Defendant GM distributed and sold the 2005 Chevrolet Cobalt and similarly designed vehicles throughout the United States of America."

GM replied: No, we didn't. Their exact words were, "This defendant denies that it distributed or sold the subject 2005 Cobalt and other similarly designed vehicles." How could GM deny it had distributed and sold a General Motors product? The answer goes back to GM's bankruptcy in 2009 and the government bailout that kept them from going under. As part of the bailout, the federal government actually bought General Motors Corporation rather than allow it to go through the normal bankruptcy process. The company then reorganized as an entirely new business entity, General Motors LLC. In fact, part of the original wording of the bailout deal the Obama administration made with GM absolved the new GM from any liability for any cars manufactured before July 1, 2009. If that provision of the deal had remained in place, GM LLC would be off the hook for any problems with any of their past products, even though the difference between General Motors Corporation and General Motors LLC was essentially in name only. They continued making the same cars in the same factories with the same employees they had before the bailout. A consortium of lawyers and consumer interest groups, of which I was a part, petitioned the Obama administration to reconsider absolving the new GM of all responsibility for the old GM's products. Thankfully they did and changed that part of the bill. However, they did absolve General Motors LLC, aka new GM, from liability from claims involving incidents before July 1, 2009. As a result, I had two pending cases on which I was working essentially wiped out by the bailout.

Two years later, GM LLC now claimed they were not responsible for a car sold by General Motors Corporation because that corporation no longer existed. Not only did they deny they sold the car, they denied that they "designed, inspected, tested, manufactured or assembled the subject 2005 Chevrolet Cobalt." In other words, they had absolutely nothing to do with this car. How then could they possibly be responsible for any problems in it? Old GM did that, not new GM.

GM also denied bearing any responsibility for the Cobalt, including our assertion that automobile manufacturers have a legal duty to "design, inspect, test, manufacture and assemble" their cars in a way that will make them reasonably crashworthy and provide a reasonable degree of safety for the occupants. While they admitted that manufacturers of automotive vehicles have certain duties and obligations, making a crashworthy car that protects its occupants was not one of them.

When it came to the 2005 Cobalt, a car they had nothing to do with but would defend anyway, they denied it had any problems. We asserted in the suit that the Cobalt is "uncrashworthy, unreasonably dangerous and unsafe for foreseeable users and occupants" for three particular reasons. First, it had a poorly designed and constructed electronic power steering system which could stop working. Second, the electrical system allowed the Cobalt to stall or lose power while driving. And third, GM failed to warn consumers and the public at large about the unsafe and defective condition of the vehicle so that people could make an informed decision before driving or riding in these vehicles. We also charged that the defective nature of the Cobalt caused Brooke's injuries and subsequent death.

GM's response: "We deny these allegations" and every other allegation we made, not that I was surprised. Claiming innocence is always a popular defense.

Their third line of defense was to claim that if there was a problem, it was not their fault. They claimed Brooke was at fault for driving too fast on a rain-slick highway. She did not "exercise ordinary care for her own safety," they wrote. On top of that, GM claimed that drivers always take on an assumption of risk for which GM could not be held responsible. That is, anytime you get behind the wheel, you know an accident is possible. GM cannot be held financially responsible for that. In addition, they declared that even if there was a problem with Brooke's Cobalt, she must have modified it in some way which then resulted in the accident. While not specifically mentioning her after-market security system, that's what they were referencing.

Finally, GM claimed that any award of punitive damages, or even our claim for punitive damages, would violate their due process rights guaranteed by the Fourteenth Amendment. How? The Cobalt was not manufactured in Georgia, and yet we had sued them in a Georgia state court. Essentially, this meant the state court had no jurisdiction in this case and therefore the lawsuit must be thrown out. Left unsaid was the assertion that if we wanted to sue, we had to do so in federal court (i.e., "so don't bother"). Once again, GM claimed innocence per the 2009 bailout agreement.

Delay, Delay, Delay

GM replied to the lawsuit right on schedule. Getting them to respond to our document requests took much, much longer. Harold Franklin called me a few days before the deadline. The call was not a surprise. "Lance," he said, "I can produce some of the documents you've requested, but your requests are pretty broad. It's going to take some time to track down everything you need. I think we're going to need at least another sixty days to come up with them."

"That's fine, Harold. I appreciate your asking. We'll give you the extension," I replied.

"We just want to be thorough in our search for everything pertinent to this case," Harold said.

"I appreciate that, Harold. Just keep me posted as we go forward." Harold and I had had variations of this conversation multiple times before. Conversations like this are a normal part of this stage of the civil justice process. Giving Harold and General Motors more time to produce documents was more than a professional courtesy. This back-and-forth is all part of the litigation dance in which one must engage. There was a very good chance that somewhere down the line, either now or in later discovery periods, I would have to file a motion to compel with Judge Tanksley. A motion to compel basically asks the judge to force one of the litigants to do what they are already required to do by law. If we had to go to those lengths at some point in the future, I wanted to be able to stand before the judge and say that we bent over backward to accommodate the other side. Only by showing her that we had exhausted all other means could we then receive a favorable ruling. And believe me, I knew from experience that that day was coming. The only question was when.

Delays are one of the major strategies defendants use in civil litigation. Most suits turn into a war of attrition where the opposition tries to wear out plaintiffs by dragging the procedure out as long as possible. When I first started practicing law, I allowed delay tactics to get to me. When defendants did not do what they were supposed to do in a timely manner, I often became quite emotional. Filled with righteous indignation, I'd lose my cool and start trying to force them to act right away. With time I realized that allowing my frustration to get the best of me played right into the opposition's hands. The more frustrated you become and the more desperation you feel, the more likely you are to make mistakes or burn out.

Eventually I learned to keep myself under control and stay focused on whatever I needed to do to keep moving the case along one step at a time. In this case, when neither Jeff Hyatt nor Chris Caruso could explain the SDM data or tell me definitively whether the electronic power steering caused the accident, I didn't get frustrated. Instead I stepped back and asked myself, *What's the next step?* In this case, the next step was filing the lawsuit to force GM to give us the information we needed. In football terms, instead of going for the long bomb down the field to try to score in one play, I focused on just moving the ball down the field three or four yards at a time. In civil actions, that means filing what needs to be filed, waiting for responses, granting extensions but making it clear that when they did respond, they had to give us the information we needed. While this approach isn't as flashy as an eighty-yard touchdown pass, it works.

GM's first sixty-day discovery extension expired at the end of August 2011. Harold and I had another phone conversation that went very much like the first. "We need more time to find the right documents," he told me.

"That's fine, Harold," I replied. "We'll give you another extension." I cannot recall if we gave them another thirty or sixty days. At some point, however, I reminded him that these delays could not go on forever. If they did not produce the documents we requested in a timely manner, we'd have to go before the court with a motion to compel.

"No, Lance, there won't be a need for that," Harold said, or something like that. I've had so many variations of this same conversation, they all run together.

While I waited for documents, I started preparing for my first deposition of a witness from General Motors. When Chris Caruso told me he could not make sense of the SDM data, he assured me that GM could. Harold produced Brian Everest as the man who could do just that. Brian was a senior consultant manager at GM who managed the team responsible for accident reconstruction. I hoped Mr. Everest could answer my questions, but I also knew I needed to find someone who could give me a completely unbiased evaluation of Brooke's Cobalt. I asked Doreen to reach out to other trial lawyers we knew who handled automotive defect cases to see who they would recommend. Doreen spoke with Cale Conley, a trial lawyer in Atlanta, who recommended Charlie Miller, a mechanic from Merigold, Mississippi. Cale added, "Charlie's the best." Little did I know that Cale's recommendation would completely turn this case around.

CHAPTER 5

The Mystery Grows

During our first phone conversation, Charlie Miller warned me that when he inspected Brooke's Cobalt, he might not find what I wanted him to find. He'd read the recall notice.

"I don't know that this could have caused the kind of accident you described to me," he said, "and I've never seen one of these lock up the steering wheel." He explained that the recall notice described a problem with the power steering not working. "That just makes the car a lot harder to steer," Charlie explained, "but it doesn't lock up the steering column itself. Now there could be some other defect we don't know about that did that. That's always possible, but we can't know for sure until we take the thing apart."

Unfortunately, Harold Franklin and GM had thus far resisted my efforts to schedule a disassembly in a timely manner. On November 29, 2011, they did their own inspection of Brooke's car. For the first time they brought in an engineer, Ebram Handy, from Detroit to take a look. Handy worked in GM's vehicle performance group. Basically, he was GM's electronic power steering system expert. Neither I nor Doreen nor anyone else from my office attended when Handy inspected Brooke's car. Since Handy did not plan on taking anything apart, I simply had one of ATS's engineers sit in for us. When I talked to ATS later, they assured me nothing new was found.

I was anxious for my own expert to get his hands on the car. After eight months of looking at Brooke's car, I was ready to get someone in there who could disassemble the steering column and anything else needed to answer these questions. I kept bringing this up with Harold. After all, with the suit filed, it was a question only of when, not if, we'd get the green light to take the steering apart. Yet Harold remained less than enthusiastic about anyone ever taking anything apart on this car. His hesitance struck me as a little out of character. We both knew that eventually the steering column would be taken apart and inspected. Yet every time I brought it up, he put on the brakes. "Listen, Lance," he'd tell me, "we're going to agree to this inspection, but I've got to figure out who at GM needs to fly down here for it, and then we'll have to coordinate their schedule with mine and yours and your expert's. I tell you what. I'll get back with you when we figure out when we have some available dates."

Of course I'd agree because my only other choice was to file a motion to compel and go before Judge Tanksley. I'd learned that you should take that step only when you've exhausted all others, which I had not. So I kept agreeing to Harold's extension requests. Then two or three weeks would go by and I'd not hear from him, so I'd call him again. He would then give me another variation on the conversation we'd already had. This was starting to feel like stonewalling.

Preliminary Judgment

I flew in Charlie Miller the first week of December 2011 to do an initial inspection of Brooke's car by himself. I was impressed with him the first time I met him. He walked into the ATS facility with a smile on his face. Even though he came recommended from trial lawyers across the country as *the* guy to unravel any mystery in an automotive case, he came across as very down to earth and humble.

He went right to work on Brooke's car. We still couldn't dismantle anything, but that didn't stop Charlie from being thorough. He started with the tires. "Now the tread on these tires, now that means something," he said with his slow Mississippi drawl. "Police report says she lost control on a wet road, which means she had to hydroplane. But y'all told me it was barely raining at the time of her accident. Hydroplaning in a light rain means the tread would have to be nearly gone, but take a look here at these tires." I bent over to take a look. "See that?" Charlie asked.

"Okay?" I said, unsure what I was looking at.

"Got good tread here. Means she didn't hydroplane. Makes me doubt she lost control because of a wet road."

I was impressed. Just by looking at the tires, Charlie made me think something other than driver error had to have caused Brooke's accident. The question was what. Because of the recall notice and the locked steering wheel, I thought the answer might lie in the electronic power steering system. Even though the engine compartment of the car had also been largely submerged for nearly an hour when the car ran into the creek, Charlie felt confident that he could tell what kind of shape it all had been in before the accident. He then compared what he found on the car to the recall notice. That's when I learned Charlie is a straight shooter. "I seriously doubt the power steering had anything to do with this accident," he said.

"What? Why?" I asked.

"I can't completely rule it out until I take it apart," he said, "but in all my years of experience, I've never seen a power steering problem cause an accident like this, especially not with the problem described in the recall. She was going straight down the highway. Her steering goes out, she's gonna keep going straight."

To say I was disappointed is an understatement. All along I claimed I wanted answers, and now I had the biggest one of all. When I filed the lawsuit, I pinned most of it on the defective electronic power steering. Now, just like that, the rug had been pulled out from under me. No power steering problem, no lawsuit.

Charlie, thankfully, was not finished. After going over the SDM data, he saw several lines that didn't make sense to him. In the precrash data, not only did the vehicle and engine speeds drop to zero three seconds before impact, but several other parameters that should have indicated something all read invalid. "Percent throttle" and "accelerator pedal position," both of which show whether Brooke's foot was on the gas pedal, read invalid, as did the antilock brake system, steering wheel angle, and vehicle dynamics control. All should have had some number. Charlie then did his own printout of the data to make sure the readings were correct. As it turned out, his printout was no different than the one we printed during the first inspection back in March.

"All right," he said, "here are the things that just aren't right in this readout. First, it says the power mode is in the accessory. Normally it should be in run. If the readout is right, her car was off at the time of the accident.

"Second, the system status shows the transmission range selector, or her gear shift, is in fourth gear, but the transmission range is in second gear."

"What does that mean?" I asked.

"With an automatic transmission, when you put it in drive, the transmission shifts into higher gears as you speed up. She was going highway speed, which means the transmission should be in fourth gear, her highest gear. The readout says hers was in second. Now, at that speed the only way the tranny is going to drop down to a lower gear is you put it there yourself by shifting from D to 2. But the readout tells me she didn't do that because the shifter never moved from drive. The transmission itself did a hard downshift like when you drive a manual transmission, drop it into a lower gear, and pop the clutch," Charlie explained.

"So what would that do to the car?" I asked.

"It could have locked up the front wheels at that speed. Do that on a wet road, that's going to be trouble," he said.

"So why would the transmission change gears like that? Is that a problem with the shifter or the transmission?"

"I'll need to study that one. Also, the speed dropped to zero on this readout three seconds before the crash when it was steady at fifty-something four and five seconds before the crash. That tells me she wasn't in a yaw or anything like that. Four seconds before the crash she was going straight down the highway. Then all of the sudden, she's crossways in the other lane."

"Yeah, the woman driving the other car said in her statement it was like Brooke's car had dropped down out of the sky all at once in front of her," I added.

"There's more going on than I can figure out just from the SDM readout. I need to come back with my own scan tools and get every computer system in this car to talk to me," Charlie said. "Like I said, the power steering most likely wasn't the culprit, but there still may be something here."

I hoped he was right; otherwise, this case had come to an end much faster than I ever anticipated. By this point, I had invested around $25,000, which did not seem like a significant amount in comparison to my firm's normal investment in a lawsuit. However, given the losses I sustained in the not too distant past and the toll those losses had taken on my personal finances, $25,000 was, in the words of my wife, Sonja, twenty-five *thousand* dollars!

I started thinking about how I should break the news to Ken and Beth. Ten months had passed since their initial appointment, and more than eight since Allstate had decided to settle with the occupants of the other car, thus negating the possibility of a lawsuit against them. Given all they'd already been through before they came to see me for the first time, I felt sick that perhaps I'd added to their pain by dragging this case out needlessly. I hoped Charlie would bring me some good news on his next inspection.

Documents Finally Arrive

After months of delay upon delay, on December 20, 2011, GM finally sent my office a CD containing the first set of documents we'd requested.

This initial batch was small, comparatively speaking, numbering in the hundreds of pages. Doreen went through each one and created a chart for the categories and the documents produced within them.

This first cache of documents all focused on the technical specifications of the Cobalt electronic power steering system, including engineering notes and drawings of the steering column. GM also included their failure mode and effects analysis (FMEA) of the power steering system. Manufacturers typically produce FMEAs as a tool for identifying potential problems before they occur. By doing so, they can also plan possible fixes in case those potential problems become actual problems. Since issues did arise with the power steering, resulting in the recall notice that started us down this path, we requested and GM supplied the FMEAs related to the power steering recall notice.

After charting the documents, Doreen went over them to decide which were important and which were not. After working with me for almost twenty years, she knows exactly what I'm looking for. Corporate defendants in product liability cases typically provide lots of documents that are not relevant, or are simply not what we need. (By the time this case ended in 2014, we received well over 100,000 pages of documents.) Defendants claim they provide so many documents to make sure they give us everything we've requested with nothing held back. At least that's what they can say to a judge. In my experience, massive document dumps often seem designed simply to overwhelm an opponent. Most small firms lack the resources to go through the thousands upon thousands of pages. In a war of attrition, this is the point where many tap out.

Once she narrowed down the important documents, Doreen read them, making notes of what other documents GM might have that were not included. She also highlighted key documents and passages before printing off hard copies for me, which she then compiled into a notebook. As a technologically challenged person, I much prefer hard copies to computer screens. I read through the key documents and Doreen's notes and used them to compile a list of witnesses I wanted to depose as well as a list of additional documents we needed GM to produce. The process is rather tedious, especially for Doreen, but in the end, it allows us to see the case with much greater clarity.

Accessory Mode

Three days before Christmas, Charlie flew back out to scan all of the various fault codes from all of Brooke's Cobalt's onboard computers. The car itself would then tell him nearly everything he needed to know about the condition of the car and all of its electrical systems, including its electronic power steering system at the time of the accident. Before returning, he also began searching for technical service bulletins, or TSBs, on the Chevy Cobalt. TSBs differ from recall notices, although both flag potential problems with a car. Recalls focus on safety issues, problems that could cause serious harm if not corrected. Consumers are contacted directly, usually by mail, during a recall. TSBs go out to dealers only to advise service technicians on non-safety-related issues that may emerge after a vehicle leaves the factory. When the mechanic at Thornton Chevrolet told Brooke she should have her shifter replaced, he did this based on a TSB. These bulletins explain how to diagnose and repair a potential problem, including what tools, techniques, and parts will be needed.

When Charlie went looking for TSBs on the Cobalt, he didn't have to look very hard because there were around two hundred of them. For a product touted at its release to compete with Toyota and Honda in terms of quality, the Cobalt had fallen well short, so much so that GM ended the line in 2010, only five years after its launch. In contrast, the Cavalier, the car the Cobalt replaced in Chevrolet's lineup, was in production for twenty-three years beginning with the 1982 model year. The TSBs gave Charlie other possible things to check out on his next inspection.

On the day of the inspection, Charlie connected his diagnostic scan tool to Brooke's car and began going through it system by system.

Unlike SDM data, which goes back only five seconds prior to the accident, fault codes remain stored in the car's onboard computer indefinitely. This allows a technician to essentially go back in time in the car's performance. When Charlie checked the electronic power steering module, he found an issue that told me we might be on to something. "The power steering isn't talking to the car's onboard computer, but that may be related to the car being submerged in the creek since the whole system is electronic," he said. "So it's hard to get an answer from the fault codes here.

"In the note Brooke wrote about the car's problems prior to taking it into Thornton Chevrolet for the stalling problem, however, she said the car was hard to turn after the car stalled. That does not happen when the car just stalls, like when the fuel system or electrical ignition or something like that makes the engine die. If the key is in the run position, the electronic steering assist still works. Steering will be normal. The only way the steering becomes hard is if you turn the key out of run and into accessory or off," he explained.

Charlie then moved on to check for any fault codes related to the engine stall which Thornton was supposed to have repaired. He shook his head and said, "As a mechanic, I typically look for long-term and short-term fuel trim. That's like a history of the engine. It tells you whether the computer has had to add extra gas to the mix going into the cylinders or if it had to take some away. That is, one way you have too much fuel pressure. The other you don't have enough. That tells you whether the fuel injectors need cleaning or if the fuel filter needs to be replaced. And those numbers don't go away once you make those repairs. They stick around like I said, a history of the engine.

"The numbers on this one all come back normal. The injectors were fine and so was the fuel filter. Brooke paid for repairs that didn't need to be done, and which did not address the problem she took the car in for in the first place," he said.

Charlie then went on to inspect the wiring, including the wiring on the aftermarket security system. Everything was normal. "A car with only 40,000 miles shouldn't have this kind of problem anyways," Charlie said. "The first thing the shop should have done was check the codes. I doubt if they did. And since they didn't, the work they did couldn't solve the problem. The engine didn't stall before Brooke took the Cobalt in to Thornton Chevrolet. The Cobalt most likely turned off like it did the night of her accident."

"When the power mode went from run to accessory," I added.

"Exactly," Charlie said.

"What would make it do that?" I asked.

"I don't know, but I'm going to try to find out."

"So if the car is off, what does that mean for the driver?" I asked.

Charlie explained to me how the Chevy Cobalt, like most cars manufactured in this century, comes equipped with a variety of safety systems designed both to prevent accidents and to protect occupants when a wreck occurs. Airbags are designed for the latter. In addition to electronic power assisted steering (which works even if the engine stalls out), Brooke's Cobalt came equipped with power antilock brakes, which keep a car from skidding when you hit the brakes hard. She also had a traction control system which gives the car added stability. However, for these systems to work, the key must be in the run position, he said. They do not continue to operate when you switch a car off or put it in accessory. Under normal circumstances, you turn a car off when you park, and a parked car doesn't need antilock brakes or traction control. No one purposefully turns off their car while traveling 58 mph down a highway.

"My scan tool confirms that all the data from the SDM is correct even though it shows up as invalid," Charlie said. "The wiring in the car appears to be intact. There's nothing physically wrong with the car that would create invalid codes on the scan tool. The only explanation is that the information is correct because the car was turned off three seconds before impact. When it did, she lost steering. She lost her antilock brakes. She lost her stability system. But before she could know any of that, the transmission dropped down into second gear because the engine just turned off. That probably locked up the front wheels and she lost control, but she could not do anything about it because she'd lost every system designed to keep the car under control."

Chills ran down my spine. "So the question is why did the car go from run to accessory?" I said.

"Right," Charlie said. "Switches are designed in such a way that the key should not just turn on its own. The switch may have been worn out because I also found her key comes out of the ignition switch no matter if the car is in park or in drive. If the lock cylinder is worn out, the key might have turned on its own if she bumped it with her knee or something like that. There's also the very unlikely chance she turned it herself, maybe out of panic. However, the numbers I see indicate she was going straight down the road prior to the car shutting off. I cannot imagine her just reaching up and turning the car off while going down a two-lane highway. Either way, there has to be some reason for the key moving from run to accessory. I'll keep digging to see what I can find."

I sensed Charlie was on to something, but he raised as many questions as he answered. Now it was my turn to dig a little deeper as well. I filed a Rule 30(b)(6) notice to take a deposition. That's the official name of the rule where I sent a notice to General Motors requesting a representative who had knowledge of SDM systems and their corresponding data reports generated in accidents. Once I made the request, GM then chose whom to present as a witness. In theory they produce the person within the company with the most knowledge of that particular system, such as the engineer who designed it. In practice, not only GM but every corporation that finds itself in this position selects someone from the company that is in essence a professional testifier.

For my first deposition, GM produced a senior consultant manager named Brian Everest. While I knew he, like most expert witnesses presented by defendants, would most likely dance around most of my questions, I planned on pressing him about the electrical system and what could cause a car to shut off like Brooke's Cobalt apparently did. He might not answer my questions to my full satisfaction, but at least it gave me a new avenue to explore. I just never expected that avenue to grow so wide.

CHAPTER 6

The Smoking Gun

Brian Everest did his best not to answer my most direct questions during our January 11, 2012, deposition. By not answering, he told me more than if he had given me some straight answers. I still didn't know exactly what caused Brooke's accident. The recall notice and locked steering wheel made me first focus on the electronic power steering system. Charlie ruled that out but also alerted me that the answer may lie in the power mode's movement from run to accessory. Neither of us had any idea how or why that had happened. Before Charlie brought the SDM data to me, I'd never heard of a car turning itself off. In my experience, worn-out locks, whether on houses or cars, usually don't turn at all instead of turning too easily.

To be honest, although I was suspicious the sudden loss of power might be the key to this mystery, I really didn't know I was on to something until Brian Everest's deposition. I didn't have some big "gotcha!" moment. Nor did I ever suspect Everest of telling an outright lie and thus perjuring himself. Instead he performed an artful dance to evade saying anything that might indicate a flaw in the design or manufacture of the 2005 Chevy Cobalt. The more he danced, the more I suspected he knew far more than he let on.

My line of questions for Brian Everest started off standard enough. The SDM data presented the biggest mystery in the case.

Everyone who had looked at it agreed on that, including those from GM who attended the initial download. Like Charlie, GM engineers found the data so perplexing that they did a second download during their November 29, 2011, inspection. Their numbers and codes didn't change from one readout to the next. I suspected I knew what that meant, so that's where I focused my line of questions for Brian Everest. Before asking about the SDM data, I started off by asking general questions about how the system works.

His answers were textbook. He told me the SDM is part of the supplemental restraint system, aka the airbags. The sensors constantly look for input; that is, the indication that the car has crashed, which means the airbags need to deploy. When a crash occurs, the sensors record the data related to the crash, going back five seconds prior to the accident.

I asked a few other questions related to how the SDM operates before moving on to the specific data from Brooke's Cobalt. "The vehicle power mode status reads 'Accessory.' What does accessory mean?" I asked.

"That's where you'd put it if you just wanted to listen to the radio, things like that," he replied.

"There's no power to the vehicle, other than the radio, and what else?" I asked.

"I'd have to look at the, I guess, the power schematics to understand what all gets powered up then," he said.

"But the engine wouldn't be running?"

"Correct," Everest replied.

I don't know if Everest or Harold Franklin, who attended the deposition on behalf of GM, understood the significance of this seemingly innocuous question, and I don't know if I fully did right then. However, this one question was the first of three crucial questions upon which this entire case ultimately rested. From the start I wanted to know what happened to Brooke Melton on the night she died. Without knowing it, Brian Everest confirmed what Charlie Miller told me after he scanned all the data from Brooke's Cobalt: Brooke wrecked her car because her car turned off. Although I still had a long way to go to be able to prove this before a jury, I knew this point was settled. Now the question was, Why did it turn off? And if the answer to that question was related to a design or manufacturing flaw in the Cobalt, the next question would be, Did GM know about it, and did they do something to stop it or could they have done something to stop it? Everything that happened in this case from this point forward revolved around those questions.

Everest was also about to reveal something whose significance I missed at the moment, but which became immensely important over the next year and a half. I asked, "What is the significance of it being in the accessory mode?"

"Just looking at the data alone, you can't tell. It would be, I guess, more important in an airbag case, because the SDM would disable the firing loops in the accessory mode," he said.

An airbag case. That's the line I didn't catch because I had no way of knowing that GM was involved in Chevy Cobalt airbag nondeployment cases. In other words, accidents where the airbag should have deployed but did not. Why did that matter? As Everest just admitted, when the ignition switch moves to the accessory mode, it turns off the airbags. That means they will not deploy in an accident, something General Motors had learned the hard way. Little did I know this was my first clue that this case went far beyond Brooke Melton and her 2005 Cobalt.

I think Everest immediately realized he'd said more than he should have because he quickly started dancing away from what he'd just said. I followed and asked more about the significance of the power mode being in the accessory position and what the data meant. He replied, "It's saying the data that's in the SDM's ring buffer at the time—well, the data that's in the SDM's—we said, you know, the data is coming into the SDM. So the data in the SDM at the time of algorithm enable was power mode accessory."

I had no clue what he just said, so I asked, "I guess I'm asking in layman's terms, does that mean when the crash occurred—when the crash first occurred, the power, the ignition, was in the accessory position?"

"It could be a reason for being in the accessory. But the data alone doesn't tell you that. It just tells you that when the crash started, it was in power mode accessory," Everest replied.

"Well, what does that mean, in power mode accessory? Doesn't that mean that the ignition is in the accessory power mode position?" I asked, stating what should have been obvious.

"Well, it's—no, that would be one cause or one reason that it could be in accessory."

"What are the other reasons?"

"I would look at the wiring," Everest said. He then answered my follow-up question by talking about looking for something that could imitate a turned key, including some kind of "wiring intrusion." Wiring issues became a consistent theme with GM over the next few months. Going back to their original response to the lawsuit, they were adamant that the Chevy Cobalt was a safe, reliable, well-built car. If some fatal flaw caused Brooke's accident, that flaw had to be caused by someone else. Soon I learned that every reference to a "wiring issue" was shorthand for placing the blame for Brooke's car shutting off entirely upon her aftermarket security system and whoever installed it.

Deflecting blame for the SDM readout saying the key was in the accessory position to something other than the switch actually being in the accessory position told me I had to be striking a nerve. I kept hitting it with more direct questions about the significance of the key being in the accessory position and how that impacted the various systems in Brooke's car. I asked, "If the vehicle power mode status is in the accessory position, is the engine control module working?"

"I'd have to look into that. I don't know right now," Everest said, evading my question.

"Electronic power steering?"

"Yes, I don't know, as I'm sitting here now."

"ABS [antilock brakes]?"

"Yes, I don't know."

"So what we know is, because I think you've talked earlier, if it's in accessory mode, it may work the radio, power windows, those types of things?" I said.

"Right. You'd have to look at the service manual, and it will show you what all is active in accessory mode," Everest said.

"And if it's inactive, that means that the moment, whatever the explanation is, whether it's in the accessory mode for whatever reason, that means the engine may not be on?"

"I would say that's possible," Everest said. Not two minutes earlier he had said the engine would be off. Now he said only that it was possible.

"And the electronics, power steering, may not be working?" I asked.

"Yes, I couldn't say for sure on the power steering. I don't know that, whether that's going to get fed with the accessory or not. Most likely not, but I'd have to look into that," Everest said.

I found it hard to believe that GM's expert, a man who'd had a part in designing these systems, would have to look at a service manual to know what happens to a car when you turn the switch from run to accessory. I also felt confident of what Everest would find when he did "look into it."

I moved to questions about the transmission. Charlie indicated this may have played a major role in Brooke's accident. The shifter was in fourth gear, but the transmission itself had dropped down to second gear. Charlie had already told me this should never happen at highway speeds. I asked Everest, "How do you explain that discrepancy?" (The discrepancy between the shifter being in fourth gear but the transmission itself in second.)

"Well, you've got an automatic transmission, so it's going to be shifting up and down. Right? So if you're in drive, you can get all kinds of stuff, anywhere from first gear to fourth gear, depending [on] what your automatic trans tells you to go into," Everest replied.

In other words, it's possible for the transmission to be in any gear at any time. I pressed him by pointing out that if you are going 58 miles an hour, the transmission should be in fourth gear. He acknowledged that would be consistent, but then he went on to tell me that the SDM takes snapshots of the car's data at one-second increments, even as data flows in constantly. "So there could be a time lag," he said. In other words, we don't know what happened in between the one-second snapshots, so the car could be jumping from first to second to third to fourth gears, and back again, but the SDM will record where it is only when it takes its snapshot. If that answer makes your head get a little cloudy, join the club. It's a classic example of walking right up to the edge of deception without actually lying.

I continued pressing, focusing my next round of questions on the vehicle speed and engine speed both registering as zero. I asked, "When [the vehicle speed] is listed as zero, obviously, the vehicle is not going zero miles an hour three seconds before the crash, right?"

Harold Franklin objected before Brian answered and said, "Well, I mean, you don't know that." He went on to explain that if the vehicle went into a side slide, it is possible the forward speed may have registered as zero although the vehicle continued to move, albeit sideways.

I finally asked, "Okay. So what's the most reasonable explanation for this speed, vehicle speed and engine speed, going from the numbers at four seconds before the crash to zero at three seconds before the crash?"

Once again Harold Franklin objected before Brian said, "I'd say you've got some wiring or power issue going on."

I felt confident there had to be more. Now the question was how to find it.

Technical Service Bulletins

On January 12, 2012, which also happened to be the day after the Brian Everest deposition, Doreen and I had a conference call with Charlie

Miller. Charlie got straight to the point. "Lance," he said, "I'm 99 percent sure I've found our answer."

"What is it?" I asked.

"I found technical service bulletins (TSBs) from December 2005 and October 2006, basically the same bulletin both times, that sound exactly like our problem. It's even called 'Information on Inadvertent Turning of Key Cylinder, Loss of Electrical System and No DTCs.' Here's what it says: 'There is potential for the driver to inadvertently turn off the ignition due to low ignition key cylinder torque/effort.'"

"Which means?" I asked.

"Low ignition key cylinder torque and effort means it turns too easily," he said. Charlie went on to explain how a car's ignition switch is connected to a lock barrel assembly. When you put the key in the ignition and turn it, you feel tension. To start the car, you press all the way forward to the crank position. When you release the key, it moves back slightly and holds in the run position. That's what makes a car lock assembly different from the deadbolt on the front door of a house. A deadbolt swings back and forth between two opposite positions. A car lock assembly has four settings and the spring-loaded plunger, which holds the key in place at each of them.

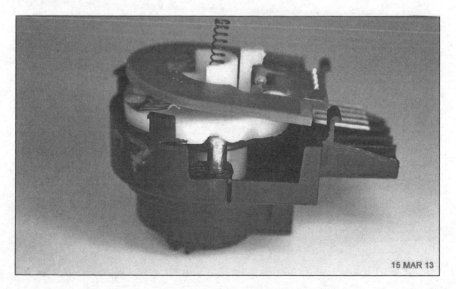

15 MAR 13

According to the Cobalt switch TSB, the tension within the key cylinder that holds the key in place was low. As a result, a driver might inadvertently turn off the switch either by hitting the key chain with a knee or by having too many objects on the key chain. The TSB stated, "The concern is more likely to occur if the driver is short or has a large and/or heavy key chain." A short driver was more likely to have the driver's seat positioned closer to the steering wheel and the steering column adjusted all the way down, thus making it more likely he or she would contact the key chain with their knee. A heavy key chain was also a problem because the added weight pulled down on the key, thus making it more likely to pop out of run and into accessory. Either way, the bulletin basically placed the blame for the problem upon the driver, not the Cobalt's key cylinder. Reading between the lines, GM's TSB basically says drivers should not be short and they shouldn't have other keys on their key rings. Sadly, I found this all too typical of the ways manufacturers try to blame customer error for the defects in their cars.

As I said, technical service bulletins are written for service managers and technicians at dealerships, not the general public. Technicians are advised when customers bring in cars complaining of a sudden engine shutoff that they should "question the customer thoroughly to determine if this may be the cause. The customer should be advised of this potential and should take steps to prevent it—such as removing unessential items from their key chain."

GM engineers also came up with an insert for the key ring that changed the key from a slot to a hole design. The key chain could not, then, move up and down the slot, and thus could no longer put extra pressure on the switch. They also replaced the key ring with a smaller one that was supposed to prevent keys from hanging so low and decrease the possibility of a short driver hitting their knee against the key chain.

"So what does this all mean, Charlie?" I asked.

"This means this problem goes way back to 2005, and the fact that they issued two bulletins, the second of which included even more cars beyond the Cobalt, means this was a problem that didn't just go away," he said.

"How did you find this?" I asked, growing excited.

"I have a system, called the Mitchell System, that gives me access to all the service bulletins car companies put out. Car makers constantly put out TSBs on their cars whenever they discover a recurring problem that's not safety related. Safety issues have to be recalled. TSBs alert mechanics to possible problems so that they can diagnose and fix them correctly when customers bring their cars in. When I got back to Mississippi, I started looking through TSBs for the Cobalt 'cause I thought for sure there had to be something there. There were somewhere around two hundred TSBs out there on this car. I searched 'engine performance' and that narrowed it down to around twenty or twenty-five. So I just scrolled through those until I hit this one. When I found it, I knew I'd discovered our problem."

"So this means GM knew these cars could just turn themselves off?" I said.

"Yep. It also means that whoever worked on Brooke's car at Thornton should have found the same TSB I did. If they had, they wouldn't have wasted their time with fuel injectors and filters," Charlie said.

"Now, Brooke went in complaining of her car stalling," I said, "and that bulletin, does it use the word 'stall'?"

"No, sir, it does not," Charlie said. "'Stall' is one of those trigger words that makes the government sit up and take notice and probably order a safety recall, so they didn't use it."

"That would make this TSB harder to find, right?" I said. "If she said her car stalled and the mechanic searched for TSBs on stalls, he would have come up empty."

"I guess that's possible, but when I looked at the fuel readouts on her car in my scan, I knew right off this wasn't fuel related. Her car didn't stall because it was starved for gas. When you see that on your scan tools, that's when you start digging through TSBs, if you hadn't already. At least that's what I do," Charlie said. "It didn't take me that long to find what I was looking for."

Charlie went on to tell me how he'd gone to a salvage yard and purchased the steering column of another 2005 Cobalt. He took it apart to study the key cylinder in action and see how it works. The cylinder switch in the steering column he took apart also had low torque. That is, it turned easily, which made him only that much more confident he'd found the problem.

"So the TSB confirms the codes on the SDM data," Charlie said. "The vehicle power mode was in accessory because that's where the key was. And the vehicle speed and engine speed were both zero because the car was off, and all that made the transmission drop down into second gear even though the car was traveling fifty-something miles an hour. Everything in the SDM readout is consistent with inadvertently turning the car off. The fact that it had happened to her just a few days before and that the place where she took it for service did nothing to address that problem tells me we've found what we've been looking for."

My heart leapt. This was the break we needed.

Charlie brought me back to earth when he said, "But this is a double-edged sword for your case. The TSB means there's a problem, but the fact that GM issued the TSB in the first place means they addressed it. Once they issue one of these things, the dealership where she had the work done should have caught it and fixed her car the way the bulletin recommends."

"And if they had?" I asked.

"Can't say for sure right now, but I'd say there's a pretty good chance that wreck never happens," Charlie said.

"And Brooke Melton would still be alive," I said.

"That's how it looks right now," Charlie said. "But to know for sure we need to do a lot more studying."

"Of the switch," I said.

"Yep, the switch," Charlie said.

After I hung up, I let the truth of what Charlie had just said sink in. It appeared that a defective ignition switch cost Brooke Melton her life, along with the sobering reality that if whoever worked on Brooke's car had pulled up the technical service bulletins for the 2005 Cobalt and taken the step of replacing her key and key ring, she would still be alive today. I couldn't help but wonder how many other Melton families were out there who had lost, or would lose in the future, a loved one because of this same defect.

CHAPTER 7

Eliminating the Variables

"We found a technical service bulletin that seems to describe what happened in our accident," I told Harold Franklin when I called him right after Charlie Miller told me about the TSB. I gave Harold the TSB title and number. "Our expert, Charlie Miller, found this because you did not produce it for us in the documents we requested. Why not?"

If my question struck a chord, Harold did not let on. "Why would we have produced that for you, Lance? This is a power steering case, not an ignition switch case. We gave you the specific documents you asked for."

"What we need are all the documents that will help us uncover what happened in this accident. The SDM data says the switch was in accessory mode. That explains all the other odd data in the SDM report. This TSB says the key in a Cobalt can inadvertently turn from run to accessory, which Charlie tells me is exactly what happened here," I countered.

"I don't see how you can prove that, Lance. Frankly, I think it is pointless to go down that path," Harold said. "You covered this in your deposition of Brian Everest. He told you what my people tell me: if the vehicle power mode went into accessory, there was probably a wiring problem that caused it. Our people have looked at this and they all think that the alarm system she had installed is probably the root of the problem. If the dealership that installed it didn't do it right, then it's going to play havoc with the rest of the systems in the car. You've seen the SDM readouts. A lot of them don't make any sense, not if the car is behaving like it was designed to. But you throw in some faulty wiring, and that could explain it all right there." The more he brought up the alarm system, the more it became clear he was trying to throw someone else under the bus to let GM off the hook.

Harold Franklin wasn't the only GM connected person talking about Brooke's alarm system. Brian Everest alluded to it by talking about wiring problems. During the car inspections with representatives from GM, someone always made a point of mentioning the security system. While I seriously doubted the system had anything to do with the accident, I had to at least take their concerns under consideration.

The state of Georgia places a two-year statute of limitations on filing a lawsuit involving an accident, including amending an already existing lawsuit by adding more defendants. My two-year window was going to close on March 9, 2012. I now faced a big decision. If we came to the end of the discovery process with GM and Thornton and somehow their people were correct about the security system, I'd have my proof that Brooke's accident had been caused by negligence, but I could not hold the people responsible accountable. DEI Holdings manufactured the security system, and Bill Heard Chevrolet, the place where Brooke bought her car, installed it. If DEI manufactured a faulty security system or if Bill Heard Chevrolet installed it wrong, and either of those actions caused this accident, I'd have an empty seat at the trial unless I amended the original suit now and added them as defendants. Even though the possibility was remote that the security system caused this accident, I could not take that chance. I added both to the complaint on March 7, 2012.

GM basically forced my hand and made me add DEI and Bill Heard to the lawsuit, but by doing so, they actually did me a favor. All along, everyone from Harold Franklin to Brian Everest to the teams of GM engineers who inspected Brooke's car all pointed to the security system and said, "There's your likely problem." By adding DEI and Bill Heard to the complaint, I could now depose their witnesses and request their documents to discover whether one of their security systems had ever caused a problem like this before. Basically, I now had a free hand to fully investigate this alarm and definitively prove, one way or another, if this was the smoking gun. GM was so adamant that the security system caused Brooke's Cobalt to go from run to accessory that I began to suspect they were using it as a smokescreen for something they did not want to talk about. Once I eliminated it, they'd have no place to hide.

More Delays

On March 21, two weeks after I amended the lawsuit, GM delivered another 11,629 pages of documented consumer complaints about the Chevy Cobalt power steering system. These were on top of the nearly 2,000 pages of documents they sent us on February 2 and February 17. This last set included transcripts of conversations between GM service representatives and customers. This was the classic case of hiding evidence under a mountain of information. When I next talked to Harold, once again requesting documents related to the Cobalt's tendency to turn itself off, he said something like, "Be reasonable, Lance. We just sent you more than 10,000 pages of documents. What more can we do?"

To which I replied, "I don't care how many documents you produced. I just want you to produce all the ones we've requested, and these are not them." We had variations of the conversation many times over the course of this case.

Harold and I also continued talking about disassembling the steering column. Jeff Hyatt told me after the first inspection back in March 2011 that we needed to take the column apart. One year later we were no closer to making that happen. When I pressed Harold, he downplayed the necessity of it. "We've inspected the car numerous times and our people, the ones who designed and built this car, all agree that the power steering wasn't the issue," was his standard response.

I kept pressing my case. "My guys tell me the only way to know for sure what role the power steering played is to take the steering column apart," I countered. "That steering wheel is locked up for a reason and we need to take it apart to find out what that reason is." That wasn't my only reason for wanting to take the steering column apart. Charlie had told me that disassembling it was also the only way to get full access to both sides of the ignition switch. Only then could we determine if the switch was simply worn out or if it had a manufacturing or design flaw.

Eventually Harold came back to me with questions about protocols for the steering column disassembly. Once again, he also brought up the security system and the car's wiring and the fact that Brooke's Cobalt had been partially submerged for maybe an hour when it came to rest in the creek in the accident. He pointed to the latter as the cause of the odd readouts in the SDM data. Harold's legal dance routine made it clear he wasn't just going to agree to the disassembly. I had to do more to establish the need. For that I went back to Charlie Miller and explained the situation to him. He told me he'd do what he could.

A couple of weeks later Charlie put together a proposed protocol for a joint inspection of Brooke's car along with GM's experts and engineers. Essentially, this inspection would serve as a precursor to a later inspection where we could finally take the steering column apart. Charlie proposed once again scanning all the car's electrical systems and inspecting the wiring harnesses along with the operation of the ignition switch. During this inspection, the procedure for disassembling the steering column would be discussed and the process agreed upon by all parties concerned.

Two months later, Harold Franklin and GM finally agreed to the inspection Charlie requested. Four engineers from GM attended, along with representatives from Thornton Chevrolet, DEI, and Bill Heard Chevrolet. I especially wanted the latter two there. Before the inspection I pulled Charlie aside and asked him to thoroughly go over everything even remotely associated with the security system. "We just need to rule it in or rule it out in front of everybody," I told him. Thankfully he did just that. He paid particular attention to how the system had been installed and determined both that it had been installed properly and that it was working as designed at the time of the accident. Although GM did not officially acknowledge that the security system did not cause the vehicle power mode to read accessory, they stopped bringing it up. Several months later they finally agreed to a dismissal of Bill Heard Chevrolet and DEI from the lawsuit.

The other positive to come out of the July 17, 2012, inspection was that at long last, GM's engineers and Charlie worked out an agreement where they would dismantle the steering column in the near future. We scheduled that inspection for August 30. Because nothing is ever simple in legal matters, we could not just say we were going to disassemble the column, have everyone gather around and watch and film it, and go on from there. Instead we worked out a plan whereby everything would be X-rayed and inspected and analyzed before the actual dismantling.

Now that that end was in sight, Charlie pulled me aside and said, "There's only so much I can do for you from here on out. I'm a mechanic. I can testify about how the steering and the ignition switch are supposed to work. I can take them apart for you and help you see what the issues are. But I can only diagnose. I cannot go into the design and manufacture aspects with authority. For that you're going to need an engineer."

When I asked Charlie whom he might suggest, he recommended Dr. Richard McSwain and his firm, McSwain Engineering, from Pensacola, Florida. When I checked out his firm, I knew Charlie had steered me in the right direction. McSwain Engineering specializes in failure analysis and accident investigation. Their labs are equipped with state-of-the-art equipment for nondestructive testing of parts and components. Dr. McSwain was very respected, especially for his work in failure analysis and accident investigation in aviation, including working for the US Navy.

When I contacted Dr. McSwain, he told me his schedule did not allow him to get involved in our case. Instead he recommended one of the engineers in his firm, a man named Mark Hood. Mark is a metallurgical engineer who specializes in nondestructive testing and failure analysis of automotive and aeronautical components. Looking back, finding Mark Hood proved again to be another providential move. Like Charlie Miller, Mark went above and beyond anything I could have expected from him. He also discovered a key piece of evidence that proved to be another turning point in the case. But I'm getting ahead of myself.

I called Mark Hood and explained where we were with the case. "We filed the case because of problems with the power steering system, but now we feel very confident that the problem lies in the ignition switch," I told him. "The problem is we need to take the steering column apart to find out what is going on with the switch, but we have no idea how long that is going to take. We're fighting to get it done as soon as possible." Mark assured me that any delays would not be a problem. Rather than wait for us to make Brooke's Cobalt's ignition switch available to him, Mark started working right away. He found another 2005 Cobalt in a salvage yard and began taking it apart and analyzing its components.

Now that I had found an engineer and lab that could do the type of analysis we needed to get answers, I called Harold Franklin to bring him up to speed on what we planned to do next. GM did not have to sign off on whomever I hired to analyze the switch, obviously, and since the car belonged to me, I could send it wherever I wanted. However, I apprised Harold of my plans as a professional courtesy. My conversations with Harold had started to change. The easy familiarity we'd always enjoyed now felt tense. When I called to tell him where the steering column would go, I could tell from the tone of his voice that this lawsuit had now registered on GM's radar in a way it had not before. In our early conversations immediately before and after I filed suit, Harold said things like, "Why do you want to do this, Lance? There's nothing there. This is going to cost you a lot of time and money for nothing." But now his tone was more serious. When I told him that I was very concerned about the ignition switch and I wanted to have it tested in light of the TSB we'd uncovered, the conversation grew very uncomfortable.

I did not know at the time that Harold was involved in two other cases involving GM ignition switches. Nor did I know that those weren't the only suits filed against GM across the country. Harold did. I also did not know what sort of paper trail there might be surrounding the two technical service bulletins GM had issued for the Cobalt and other models that shared its platform, but I knew there had to be one.

While Charlie got himself ready to finally dismantle the steering column, I began working on my next set of discovery requests I planned to file as soon as we could isolate Brooke's switch and begin to test it. I knew we had to be getting close to the truth. The other side had to feel like the walls were closing in. I just needed to give them one more firm push.

CHAPTER 8

GM Finally Takes Notice

After a year and a half of buildup, the actual disassembly of the steering column on Brooke's Cobalt at ATS turned out to be rather anticlimactic. Rather than a big reveal, the process felt like jumping through one more hoop on our way to getting down to the real problem with Brooke's car: the ignition switch. Charlie Miller flew in from Mississippi for the steering system disassembly, while GM had four engineers in attendance, including Ryan Jahr, who was there at the first inspection, and Ebram Handy, the man who designed the Cobalt steering column. Harold attended, as did I.

Charlie did the actual removal of the steering column and all its components. Within minutes he cleared up the mystery of why the wheel was locked. When he removed the electric motor at the base of the steering column, water drained out. "That's why it was locked up," Charlie said. "Had nothing to do with the recall or anything else. The wreck did it. It froze up when the car went into the creek."

Harold looked around at his team with an "Aha" smile, but I didn't think anything of it. The suit I filed claimed the Cobalt was unsafe not only because it had an "inadequately designed and constructed" electronic power steering system that could result in the loss of power steering assist but also because it had "an electrical system which allows the Cobalt to stall or lose power while driving." Charlie had told me back in December that the electronic power steering system had not caused this accident. The disassembly only confirmed what we already knew. Now that we had the steering column out of the car, we could do the kind of analysis of the switch that would allow us to make a final determination about its role in Brooke's accident.

After Charlie finished removing the steering column and its components, the GM reps took multiple photographs from a variety of angles. Then we had it X-rayed before boxing it up to go to McSwain Engineering. At this time Charlie also determined the shifter had nothing to do with the accident, which was important, particularly for Ken, but not for the case. Like I said, after a year and a half of debate and delays over taking the steering assembly apart, this moment was very anticlimactic, but that was fine with me. The real drama was about to happen.

We Can Settle This

On September 13, 2012, two weeks after the steering column disassembly, I filed a second set of interrogatories and requests for the production of documents. Harold had criticized me before for being too general in my document requests. I was quite specific this time around. Among other things, I asked GM to "identify every lawsuit, claim or complaint that has been made against GM wherein it was alleged that an injury or death resulted from a problem related to Technical Service Bulletin 05-02-35-007." It was the legalese equivalent of a punch in the nose.

A few days later Harold Franklin called. He said something like, "This new set of interrogatories and documents requests is so broad and is going to take so long to sort through; this thing, Lance, it's just going to drag out forever. Your clients are nice people and they've been through so much already. I'd hate to see them endure even more. Why don't you and I sit down and talk about how we can mediate this case?"

GM was ready to talk about settling the case. As the plaintiff's counsel, settling before going to trial is often an attractive option. As I learned the hard way in my very first trial, juries are unpredictable. I've lost more than one case where I felt like the evidence was overwhelmingly in our favor. However, I actually relished the thought of this particular case going to trial. The discovery process was far from over, but I felt if we kept going in the direction we were headed, we'd have a very strong case to present before a jury. As a trial lawyer, I love that part of my job.

"I'll talk to my clients and let you know what they want to do," I told Harold.

A few days later Ken and Beth came to my office. We sat down and I brought them up to date on where we stood with the case and the investigation. Rather than lead with Harold's offer to mediate, I led with what I knew Ken most needed to hear. "The shifter had nothing to do with Brooke's accident. If she'd had the work done the mechanic recommended, it wouldn't have made any difference one way or another," I said.

It appeared a weight lifted off of Ken's shoulders. "Do you know what did cause it?" he asked.

"Not in a way that we can prove in court, not yet at least, but everything we've found so far points to the ignition switch," I said. In one of our regular meetings a few months earlier, I'd told them about the technical service bulletin regarding the ignition switch. "Now that we have the steering column out of the car, we can test the switch and that should give us some answers. I've also requested more documents from GM related to the TSB they issued, and I've also asked for them to identify every lawsuit, claim, or complaint that's been made where someone was injured or killed in an accident connected to this TSB."

"Do you think there have been others?" Beth asked. The thought that other families may have gone through what they'd experienced left her visibly shaken.

"I'd say there's a very good chance of it. We should know soon enough." I paused for a moment, then added, "There's something else.

GM has asked us to consider going to mediation to settle this now rather than continuing the discovery process and possibly going all the way to trial."

Ken and Beth looked at one another for a moment, then Beth asked, "What do you think, Lance?"

"I think the timing of their offer is very curious. As long as we were talking about the power steering, mediation never came up. As soon as we asked for documents related to the ignition switch, they immediately asked for mediation," I said.

"You think they have something to hide?" Ken asked.

"I'd say there's a whole lot more for us to discover. You should also be aware that settlements always carry a nondisclosure agreement. That means everything we've discovered thus far will be sealed."

"But if there's something wrong with the Cobalt, people need to know it. And shouldn't GM have to issue a recall?" Ken asked.

"That's up to NHTSA, the National Highway Traffic Safety Administration. GM is supposed to self-disclose when there's a safety issue that may warrant a recall. They haven't done that with the Cobalt, and we can't do it for them, especially not after signing a non-disclosure agreement. This is your case and your decision, but I think we need to continue with this and see where it leads," I said.

"Lance, whatever you think is the right thing to do," Ken said as Beth nodded in agreement. "We didn't get into this for money."

"I believe the right thing to do now is just to press on and try to figure out as much as we can about what GM knew and when they knew it. We can circle back after that and make a decision about whether we should agree to mediation. Right now, we need to continue to pursue this," I said.

"Then that's what we'll do," Ken said.

Later that day I called Harold and told him my clients wanted to continue to pursue the case. While he didn't come out and say it, I could tell he was not pleased with our decision. Once I later learned the scope of the other lawsuits in which GM found itself because of the Cobalt ignition switch, I imagined Harold had to be screaming at them, telling them to do everything they could to get the Meltons to settle as quickly as possible. That was something we had no intention of doing. As far as I was concerned, I planned to take this all the way to a jury trial.

We Object

A short time after we declined the offer to mediate the lawsuit, GM filed its responses to our interrogatories and document requests. They began by trying to redefine the lawsuit. They wrote, "GM LLC understands plaintiff's defect claims to involve a claimed electric power steering malfunction allegedly resulting from the condition contained in GM LLC's Product Safety Recall Bulletin #10023." A list of all the vehicles and model years using this power steering system then followed. This was followed by, "GM LLC objects to producing documents for any other vehicles that are outside of this scope because such requests are overly broad, unduly burdensome, not reasonably limited in time or scope to the allegations regarding the subject 2005 Chevrolet Cobalt, are not relevant, and will not lead to the discovery of admissible evidence." In essence, GM was saying they were shocked—*shocked!*—that questions had been raised about a technical service bulletin related to the ignition switch when this was nothing more than a power steering lawsuit.

In response to our specific interrogatories, GM included language describing the search parameters they would use to find the pertinent documents. Each response included the same language about our demands being overly broad, unduly burdensome, not reasonably limited in time or scope to the 2005 Cobalt, not relevant, and unlikely to lead to admissible evidence. To that they also added, "GM LLC further objects to the Interrogatory to the extent it asks for information protected from disclosure by the attorney-client privilege and/or the work product doctrine." The latter refers to material prepared by GM's lawyers for their defense in anticipation or actual defense of litigation.

Basically, all of this was GM's way of saying through their attorneys that they would look for any documents that might be there if they had to, but the judge should not force them to do so because these requests were unreasonable. I felt confident Judge Tanksley would deny their objections. She had a well-earned reputation as a judge who doesn't put up with withholding relevant evidence.

After another delay I called Harold. "What's the status with the documents we've requested?" I asked.

"My client is working on it, but you have to give us more time. Your requests are broad, and we don't know exactly what you are asking for," he replied.

"Come on, Harold. The document request is very clear. We're not asking for the moon, just the documents around the December 2005 and October 2006 TSBs. That's pretty specific."

He then said something along the lines of how large a corporation General Motors is and how many people from all across the company work on a car line and how many of their components are outsourced and how they weren't even making Cobalts anymore, which further complicated everything.

"We've done this before, Harold. You know what your client needs to produce. We can't wait forever," I said.

"Just a little more time," he said.

"Okay," I said.

But a little more time went by and still no documents were produced. October turned into November and November turned into December. Finally I told Harold, "Enough is enough. We've given you time. You haven't given us what we need. You haven't given us anything related to the ignition switch. You've left me no choice but to file a motion to compel," I said.

"Come on, Lance. You don't have to go that far," Harold replied.

"Then get your client to produce the documents we requested," I said. "If they don't, I'm filing. Nothing else has moved your client to do what they are supposed to do. Maybe this will."

"Let me see what I can do," Harold said.

I had a pretty good idea what the result was going to be. I went ahead and filed the motion to compel on December 7, 2012.

The Haymaker

Tension hung in the air the next time I saw Harold less than a week after filing the motion to compel. He barely made eye contact with me when he and Ebram Handy walked into McSwain Engineering's Florida lab for a test of the ignition switch from Brooke's Cobalt. Along with the attorney from Thornton Chevrolet, he stood on the opposite side of the room from me and Charlie Miller, like boxers in their corners waiting for the bell to ring. It was as though an invisible line had been drawn across the floor, because they never moved any closer to our side of the room, and we didn't move closer to theirs.

"Okay, let's get started," Mark Hood said. "I will follow the protocol everyone agreed to ahead of time." He held up a torque screwdriver which measured force as it turned. "I will use this to turn the switch from the Melton Cobalt. It will give me a readout of how much force is needed to turn it to the various positions. The switch itself will be placed in this holder and connected by wires to a light box that will light up in green for run, yellow for accessory, and red for off. Does anyone have any questions?"

I did not because Charlie Miller and I had flown in the day before so that Mark could go over the entire procedure with me. He could not test the Melton switch without Harold and the others from GM being present. Instead he went through the entire testing procedure for me using both brand-new and used exemplar switches he'd picked up at the salvage yard. We talked about GM's own torque specifications for the switch. Whether or not these exemplar switches met that did not matter during the test run the day before the official testing. Not yet at least. The only numbers that mattered were those from the Melton Cobalt switch.

Neither Harold nor Ebram, nor anyone on their side, had any questions either.

Mark then unsealed the box into which the Melton switch had been placed back in August when Charlie Miller removed it from Brooke's Cobalt. Harold and Ebram moved in close and peered over his shoulder as Mark placed the switch assembly and housing into the holder he'd designed and hooked up the wires to the light box. Mark then took a sharpie and marked the crank, run, accessory, and off positions on the holder so that everyone in the room could clearly see which position the key was in. A photographer and videographer recorded his every movement.

Mark inserted the torque screwdriver into the switch and said, "I'll go up to crank, that should have the most tension." A light turned on. "Now run," he said as he released the key, allowing the tension spring within the lock assembly to pop the switch into the run position. A green light came on. Mark snapped a photograph of the readout on the torque screwdriver. "And now accessory," he said. A yellow light came on. He took another photograph of the readout. "Back to run," he said. The green light came back on. Once again, Mark took a photograph of the readout. He repeated the procedure several times.

"So we're consistently getting a reading of 15.66 ounce inch to turn the switch from run to accessory or back again," Mark said. He typed the numbers into his computer. "On the Newton centimeter scale, that gives us a reading of 11.06."

I glanced over at the GM side. Ebram Handy's eyes appeared to grow wide. He leaned over and whispered something to Harold, who quickly replied. They moved back away from us like a football team in a huddle and kept talking in hushed tones. Their conversation went back and forth hurriedly for a few moments.

I didn't have to hear them to know what they were talking about. In the documents GM had already produced, they had disclosed the force to turn the key should be 20 N-cm, plus or minus 5. At the absolute worst, Brooke's switch should not register any lower than 15

N-cm. It didn't come close. I knew we'd found our smoking gun, the cause of Brooke's accident, and so did the team from GM, although neither of us said a word about it. We still didn't say a word across the invisible line on the floor about anything.

"I also have an exemplar switch with me that I took out of a 2005 Cobalt," Mark said. "I'm going to test it now to see how it compares." He placed it inside of the housing from Brooke's car and went through the same process with the exemplar switch. The numbers were close to what we found in Brooke's switch.

"For comparison's sake, I'd also like to test a brand-new replacement switch I bought. It's the same switch, same part number, same manufacturer, Delphi," Mark said. He then placed the new switch into the Melton housing and repeated the test he'd done with the previous two switches. "Hmm, that's interesting. The tension, or the torque required, it's double that of the other two." He repeated the test. "Yeah, exactly double."

I looked over at Harold and his team. Ebram Handy appeared agitated.

"I expected some difference because of the age of the other two switches. The springs holding the detent plunger in place lose tension over time, but I'd never expect it to be half," Mark said. "I'll keep digging and see what I can find out."

No one from GM had anything to add. Later, after the testing was complete, they gathered together in a corner of the lab. While I was too far away to hear what they were saying, Ebram Handy appeared to be quite animated as he spoke with the team of lawyers. The day we removed the steering column from the car lacked drama, but this day more than made up for it.

I flew back to Atlanta later that day. Harold called me the next morning to tell me that GM had agreed to give us more documents. "But we're going to continue to assert our objections," Harold added. "Even so, I don't see any reason for you to continue with your motion to compel."

"Let's see what they've given us first," I said. Harold's eagerness to get me to drop the motion to compel only confirmed what I already suspected. Any doubts I might have had about GM's knowing more than they let on about the Cobalt ignition switch had long since disappeared. They had secrets I was determined to bring to light. This suit had already dragged out for nearly two years now. From experience, I knew the pace was about to pick up in a very big way.

CHAPTER 9

Closing In

"You are not going to believe what I just found," Doreen said as she walked into my office a day or two after GM sent us the first set of documents connected to the Cobalt ignition switch on December 13, 2012. "They knew this switch was bad back in 2004. Take a look."

She handed me a copy of a GM Problem Resolution and Tracking System (PRTS) report. PRTS was an internal procedure GM went through when a problem with a product cropped up. The PRTS team, which included engineers and other executives, studied the problem and were supposed to come up with a solution before they closed the report, in theory at least. Before the PRTS team is even formed, the problem is assigned a severity level between 1 and 4. Code 1 is a possible safety or regulatory problem which will stop the car from being built. Code 4 is just an annoyance that needs to be improved upon. The Cobalt ignition switch was a Code 3, or something someone should have checked out the next time they happened to take their car into their Chevy dealer.

"According to the PRTS report, a GM employee named Gary Altman drove a Cobalt on October 29, 2004, and the car shut off when he bumped the key," Doreen said. We later learned that Mr.

Altman was the program engineering manager responsible for the design and development of the Cobalt.

"The car shut off on him?" I responded.

"Yes, but there is a lot more you are going to find interesting," Doreen responded.

"Let me see the report," I said. It made for fascinating reading. The initial complaint which resulted in the report said, "Vehicle can by keyed off with knee while driving." This complaint designation alone proved that, as early as October 2004, GM knew that the keys in Cobalts could rotate from the on to accessory or off position and cause the cars to stall during ordinary driving conditions.

The report also contained a "Root Cause Analysis," which described the results of GM's investigation. The GM engineers concluded two things might cause the key to turn. First, the ignition switch had low torque, meaning it would too easily turn from the run position even when the driver did not intend it to turn. Second, the key insert was too low on the steering column, meaning the driver's knee would impact the key and key chain during ordinary driving conditions.

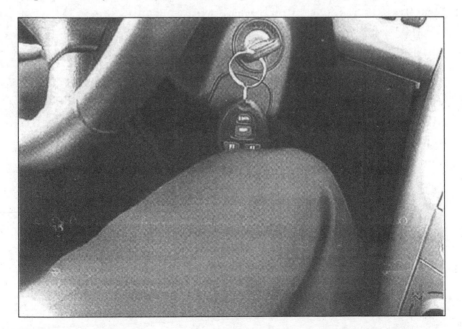

Having identified the problem, the report discussed potential solutions. The first solution was to increase the ignition switch torque. This is when we first learned the name of the GM engineer who designed the ignition switch, Ray DeGiorgio. Mr. DeGiorgio told Gary Altman and the other engineers it was impossible to change the ignition switch because it was fragile and further changes could lead to mechanical and/or electrical problems. Altman and the others accepted Mr. DeGiorgio's statements and did nothing to verify his claims.

Another GM engineer, David Trush, proposed another solution—a change in the design of the key. The torque in the ignition switch would remain the same, but the key design change would make it less likely the key would turn. His analysis showed that this solution would cost somewhere around fifty cents per car and take about twenty weeks to implement. If accepted, the solution could have been implemented by August 1, 2005. (Brooke Melton bought her Cobalt on August 30, 2005, which meant GM could have made a safer key available to her at the time of purchase.) The GM engineers then presented their findings and the proposed solutions to two high-level committees known as CPIT (Cockpit Program Integration Team) and VAPIR (Vehicle and Process Integration Review).

I was dumbfounded by what I read next in the report. These committees turned down Mr. Trush's solution because the "lead time (twenty weeks) was too long, and the cost (fifty cents per vehicle) was too high." The committees then concluded these solutions did not represent "an acceptable business case." This was GM speak, meaning, "We don't want to spend the money to fix the problem, not even fifty cents."

I had seen many incriminating documents produced by corporate defendants, and this report was one of the worst. It proved not only that GM engineers and executives knew about the defect before Brooke bought her new Cobalt on August 31, 2005, but also that they rejected a fifty-cents-per-car solution which, if implemented, would have been available when Brooke bought her Cobalt. Simply put, GM made a business decision to put profits over safety, just like Ford had done with the Pinto back in the 1970s.

The November 2004 PRTS was the first of many between 2004 and 2009 that dealt with the Cobalt's ignition switch. All described the very problem Brooke reported before she took her car into Thornton Chevrolet. None of them ended with a definitive fix for the problem, a fix that would have saved Brooke Melton's life. Instead it appeared that each PRTS team at GM just kicked the can down the road, hoping the problem would eventually go away, especially after GM ended the Cobalt line after the 2010 model year. We found other documents where changing the key from a slot to a hole was discussed but never implemented. While not a perfect solution, the change would have at least reduced the likelihood of the car turning itself off. Rather than change the key, GM issued the TSB where customers who complained could receive a snap-in plug for their key that eliminated the slot at the top, making it a single hole instead. Of course, for many customers, by the time they realized they had a problem, it would be too late. My blood was starting to boil.

Altogether, we received nearly 3,000 pages of documents. We discovered some vital information we did not have before. For one, we learned the name of the man who designed the Cobalt switch, Ray DeGiorgio. We immediately started working on trying to depose him. Other key names came out, including Gary Altman, who was over the development of the Cobalt, and Steve Oakley, who was the brand quality manager for the Cobalt when it was first launched.

We might have learned more, but unfortunately, many of the documents we received had been heavily redacted. Even so, we found a disturbing trend when it came to complaints about the Cobalt switch. Apparently General Motors did not regard a car turning off while traveling at highway speeds to be a safety concern. Instead, they referred to it as a "customer convenience issue." GM carried this same argument into their communication with the National Highway Traffic

Safety Administration. In their correspondence with NHTSA, GM described the Cobalt problem as a moving stall, using the same terms one might use to describe a car dying when it runs out of gas or when it has trouble running on an extremely cold morning.

The idea that this was not a safety issue became the company line. They carried it into public interviews when the switch issue was raised. Tucked away in the packet of documents, we found a June 19, 2005, article by Jeff Sabatini for the *New York Times*. Sabatini's wife lost power more than once in the brand-new Cobalt GM supplied him for a review test drive. Alarmed, Sabatini contacted GM, where he talked with Alan Adler, a GM manager for safety communications. Adler explained away the problem by reassuring Sabatini that intermittent stalling was not a safety issue because "the Cobalt is still controllable. The engine can be restarted after shifting to neutral." Then came what I believed must have been the company line from the time this problem first arose: "Ignition systems are designed to have on and off positions, and practically any vehicle can have power to a running engine cut off by inadvertently bumping the ignition from the run to accessory or off position."[1]

This customer convenience issue apparently impacted a lot of customers because we received page after page of documented complaints of inadvertent shutoffs that came into GM, including a large number of buybacks. That is, customers experienced the ignition switch problem often enough that GM had to buy their cars back under lemon law legislation. Many complaints included stories of drivers nearly losing control of their cars or coming close to having an accident. "I thought I was going to die," peppered many of these stories. Missing, however, were customer names and places. We had these stories, but no context. Nor did GM include anything about how the complaints were rectified outside of the buybacks.

The phrase "customer convenience issue" gnawed at me, as did "acceptable business case," both of which were GM's excuse for doing nothing. The more I read, the more I was also struck by how incomplete the documents were. Not one document mentioned any accidents caused by the issue, much less claims of injuries or death or property damage. Our interrogatories specifically asked for that information, yet we did not receive even one.

Not only was the context missing for customer complaints, the same was true for many of GM's internal investigations into engine stalling. Several referred to photographs or charts which were conspicuously absent from the documents we received. The document request we filed asked for all documents connected to the technical service bulletin about the faulty ignition switch, not a carefully selected smattering of documents. Many of the documents we received that discussed possible solutions had been redacted. We could not see all of the projected benefits, concerns, lead time, and cost increase the proposed solution may have incurred. On top of this was the fact that every document I received had been produced between 2004 and 2009, as if the problem suddenly went away on January 1, 2010.

Equally frustrating was the absence of the design drawing for the 2005 Cobalt. GM supplied us with drawings for a 2008 Cobalt and a Saturn Ion, but nothing for the car at the center of the lawsuit. The drawings we received lacked technical specifications for the force required to move the key from off to on and back again. We needed those specs. GM also failed to supply any documentation of the way in which they tested the Cobalt switch before sending it out into production. It seemed obvious enough to me that the low torque in Brooke's ignition switch had to be the rule, and the other the exception, since so many instances of the key inadvertently turning had been reported. Without the testing documentation, I had no way of proving this.

On top of everything else, I was incredulous at the way in which General Motors tried to keep the problem with the Cobalt as low-key and secretive as possible even though the earliest reviews of the car mentioned the car stalling. I was surprised GM actually included these reviews in documents they sent us, but they did, and the information within them was damning.

In addition to the *New York Times* article referenced above, Gary Heller of *The Daily Item* in Sunbury, Pennsylvania, did a review of the Cobalt in May 2005. His engine shut off four times over the course of his weeklong test drive. In his review, he wrote, "I have never encountered anything like this in 37 years of driving. I hope I never do again." His most scathing line came at the end of his review where he wrote, "The standard goodies make [the Cobalt] a tempting pick, but I'd look hard at the distance between your knee and the ignition switch before making the final decision."[2]

Christopher Jensen of Cleveland's *The Plain Dealer* sarcastically addressed GM's claim that a Cobalt can be controlled when the engine turns itself off and easily restarted by slipping it into neutral. He wrote, "So, if you're whisking along at 65 mph or trying to pull across an intersection and the engine stops, that's what you do. Only a gutless ninny would worry about such a problem. Real men are not afraid of temporary reductions in forward momentum."[3]

The fact that the news media as a whole did not pick up on the problems with the Cobalt did not completely surprise me. A poor review does not make the front page of the *New York Times*. Deaths, however, do. I could not help but believe Brooke Melton had not been the first person who died as a result of the Cobalt ignition switch. GM had to have accident and death claims. If so, they seemed to want to keep them hidden. I knew someone who just might be able to uncover them, a man named Sean Kane.

Sean is founder and president of Safety Research and Strategies, an organization that does research and analysis on injuries associated with product hazards. He has a knack for uncovering secrets buried in government databases. In 2000 he was instrumental in revealing the dangers of Ford Explorers equipped with Firestone tires, a case which led to congressional hearings and the passage of the Transportation Recall Enhancement, Accountability, and Documentation Act. His research also helped uncover the problem of Toyotas that suddenly accelerated without the driver pressing on the gas.

I called Sean and filled him in on the basics of the Melton case. "GM has sent us a load of documents which show a widespread problem and lots of consumer complaints, but there aren't any crashes. We have consumers who say they almost died after their car stopped, but that's it. I can't find anything more than near misses."

"I'll do a search and see what I can come up with," Sean said.

Moving Forward, Getting Nowhere

Harold called me not long after his office sent over GM's first set of ignition switch documents. "I assume you are going to withdraw your motion to compel now," he said.

My answer was blunt and to the point. "Harold, I am not, for two reasons. First, you did not withdraw the objections you listed in your first response to my second set of interrogatories. How do I know you've given me everything if you continue to object? If you withdraw your objection and say you've given me everything, then I can withdraw my motion to compel."

"You know I can't do that," Harold replied.

"Then neither can I withdraw my motion until you give me everything. And that's the second reason I cannot withdraw my motion. There's no way GM has sent me everything because there aren't any documents after 2009. I don't have a single investigation report or customer complaint or accident report between 2010 and today. Did all the investigations just stop? I mean, what happened?"

"Lance, we've given you everything we've got. That's it. There is no more," Harold said.

"Fine. I understand that. I guess Judge Tanksley is just going to have to sort this all out. You can stand before her and tell her you've given us everything. When you do, then that will be that." I paused for a moment and chose my next words very carefully. "I have to be honest with you, Harold. I don't trust GM when they say this is everything. I don't trust them one bit."

Harold seemed to grow upset. "This doesn't have to go that far," he said.

"Yeah, I think it does," I replied.

Harold and I did not talk again until after the Christmas holidays. Judge Tanksley's court gave us a February 7 date for a hearing on my motion to compel. A week or so into the new year, Harold called again. "I have more documents for you," he said.

"Are accident reports and injury claims included?" I asked.

"We don't have any of those," he replied.

"There haven't been any accidents or injuries connected to Cobalts suddenly turning themselves off while speeding down the road?"

"We have no record of such claims," he replied.

"Come on, Harold. Do you honestly expect me to believe that?" I asked.

"Whether you do or don't is up to you, Lance," Harold said. "We've overnighted the documents to you. You'll have them tomorrow."

True to his word, a second set of documents arrived at my office on January 14. Unfortunately, they, like the first set we received on December 13, had been heavily redacted.

Harold called again. We had another variation of the same conversation we'd had two or three times already. He asked if I was ready to withdraw the motion to compel since we had more documents. My answer had not changed. Another set of redacted documents arrived on January 17, the majority of which dealt with warranty claims. Another conversation with Harold followed. As before, my position had not changed. We still had not received any documents identifying "every lawsuit, claim or complaint that has been made against GM wherein it was alleged that an injury or death resulted from a problem related to Technical Service Bulletin 05-02-35-007 and 05-02-35-007A." Harold again reassured me that they didn't produce any such documents because there weren't any to produce. I remained skeptical. As it turned out, my skepticism was well founded.

Amy Rademaker

"I've got it," Sean Kane said when he called me a couple of weeks before the motion-to-compel hearing. "I found what you are looking for on the Special Crash Investigation section of an NHTSA website."

"What is it?" I asked.

"I just sent you an accident report from Wisconsin where two girls were killed in a 2005 Cobalt. The car went off the road and hit a tree. The front airbags did not deploy and the girls died. Their names were Amy Rademaker and Natasha Weigel. A trooper in the Wisconsin State Patrol's Technical Reconstruction Unit, Keith Young, investigated the accident and determined the ignition switch was in the accessory position rather than run when the car hit the tree. That's why the airbags did not deploy. They don't fire when the car is off. Trooper Young also found five complaints with NHTSA of '05 Cobalts turning off while being driven, and he connected those and the accident to GM's October 2006 TSB on the switch," Sean said. "He determined the car was traveling 38 at the moment of impact."

"They should have survived that if their airbags had deployed," I said.

"Exactly. And get this. According to Trooper Young's report, the crash speed did not match the vehicle speed data from the SDM, just like in your case. He surmised that was probably due to power loss."

"So the SDM data didn't make sense until they connected the dots to the switch being off, just like Brooke," I said.

"Exactly. And the accident happened the day before GM issued their amended October 25, 2006, TSB on the ignition switch," Sean said.

I was excited and disgusted and angry all at the same time. I knew GM had been lying to me when they said there weren't any accident claims to report. We learned that Trooper Young had spoken with an NHTSA representative in November 2006 about his findings. NHTSA then conducted the special crash investigation. And then did nothing. They should have ordered a recall after the Rademaker accident, but they just buried their head in the sand and chose to ignore a clear public safety issue. To me, that made NHTSA complicit. I was not entirely surprised. My past experience with NHTSA has left me less than confident of their oversight of the automobile industry, not when NHTSA staffers will leave the agency and go to work for the very industry they were charged with regulating. More about that later.

I thanked Sean, then called Harold Franklin. "I just sent you something," I said.

"What's that?" Harold asked.

"An accident investigation report from a state trooper in Wisconsin about a girl who died in a 2005 Cobalt, Amy Rademaker. The trooper determined the key was in the accessory position. Same kind of odd readouts in the SDM data as us—only in this one, two girls died because the airbags did not deploy. Airbags don't deploy when the key is off."

A moment of silence followed. Finally Harold said, "Thank you for sending this to me. I didn't know about this."

"Look," I said, "I'm tired of playing games, Harold. You tell me there are no incidents with claims of injury or death. I just gave you one where two girls died. You say you didn't know about it. Okay. I'm fairly certain someone at GM knew. The trooper sent his report to NHTSA. They would have contacted GM immediately. We both know that."

"I'm going to look into it," Harold said.

My patience was starting to wear thin, but I didn't want to burn any bridges with Harold. "Listen, I could have embarrassed you by holding on to this until the motion-to-compel hearing, but I didn't because we've always had a good relationship. I know GM knows about the Rademaker case, Harold. And you know it too. Clearly, this should have been produced to me and it wasn't. There's got to be more," I said.

"I appreciate you telling me about this ahead of time, Lance. I'm going to make some calls and I'll get back with you," Harold said.

I bit my tongue and said, "Thanks, Harold, I appreciate that." I might have said more, but I knew I didn't have to, not with the motion-to-compel hearing right around the corner.

Motion-to-Compel Hearing

Three days before we were scheduled to appear before Judge Tanksley, Harold called me back. "We found more documents a couple of days ago while preparing Ebram Handy for his deposition," he said. "He told us about some documents I wasn't aware of because they are part of an ongoing investigation of an airbag nondeploy incident. We didn't think they were relevant because your case doesn't involve airbags, but I'm going to send them to you anyway. Since we are going to produce them, there's no reason to go ahead with the motion-to-compel hearing."

"It's too late for that, Harold. We're going to have the hearing. I cannot cancel it based on a promise of documents I don't have and have no idea what's even in them," I said. "No, I want the judge to rule on your objections and then order your client to produce all responsive documents. I don't think GM has taken this seriously. This is the only way I know of to get them to."

Three days later, on February 7, 2013, the two of us appeared before Judge Tanksley. As the one filing the motion, I spoke first. I went straight to the point. "This is a case about Brooke Melton," I said as a photograph of Brooke filled the courtroom video screen. "She was a young pediatric nurse at the time of her death, and I'm going to talk to you a little bit about what happened to Brooke because that gives the—will hopefully give you—an understanding, Your Honor, of why this information is critical and we need it, the information documents that have not been produced yet."

I then talked about Brooke buying her car all while GM knew there was a problem with the Cobalt ignition switch but chose to do nothing about it. I went down the line of what we'd uncovered, beginning with Gary Altman having a Cobalt shut off on him during an early test drive. I also focused on how GM determined fixing it was going to be too expensive and take too long. "In other words," I said, "they knew this, and when they sold the vehicle to Brooke, they hadn't fixed the ignition switch, even though they knew back in '04 and early '05 that there was a problem. But for business reasons, they chose not to fix it."

After taking Judge Tanksley through how GM eventually issued a technical service bulletin, which Thornton did not bother to find even though it applied directly to the problems Brooke had with her car, I went into the accident itself. "She's driving down the road, and whatever happened—she bumps it with her knee, it shuts off just because the torque is too low. All of a sudden, it's a rainy night on Highway 92, she's driving down the road—pow, the engine goes off. She loses power steering, she loses antilock brakes, she's in an emergency situation. And she loses control of her vehicle."

I recounted all of this to keep the attention on Brooke Melton. "She lost her life because of GM's recklessness. Therefore, it only makes sense that we should have access to any other documents GM has regarding other accidents that resulted in injury or death. But GM won't produce them. So as far as incidents, lawsuits, claims, and complaints, they say there are none and what they produced is this warranty claims data. For the most part, this is useless to us," I said.

"Well, fortunately," I said as I got to the heart of my argument, "we found information from other sources which shows GM is not telling the truth." I then went through the information GM had hidden for so long. "Just overrule the objections and compel them to fully respond to our discovery on these limited issues that are part of the motion to compel," I concluded.

Harold made his case against dismissing their objections by going back to the idea that this was originally a power steering case. Now, he said, our defect theories had shifted to the ignition switch, implying that we were grasping at whatever we could find to blame GM for Brooke Melton's accident. Then, addressing the specific requests we'd made, he said that GM had produced all the documents they were able to turn up within their search parameters. He also pointed to the fact that they had produced more than 19,000 pages of documents for us already.

The judge questioned him on the search parameter question, essentially asking why they didn't use better search terms so that they might find the right documents. Her position basically came down to not caring what parameters they had used, only that they produce the documents they were legally obligated to produce.

Six days later, Judge Tanksley handed down a decision overruling GM's objections and ordering them to produce the documents we sought by February 28, 2013. GM delivered on the deadline, and not a day before.

On March 18, 2013, we amended the lawsuit and specifically cited the faulty ignition switch as the product defect which caused Brooke Melton's death. This was the nightmare scenario Harold had hoped to avoid. But it was too late for that. I thought I had an over-whelmingly compelling case. It was about to get even stronger.

CHAPTER 10

The Final Piece

In between the motion-to-compel hearing and amending the lawsuit to focus upon the ignition switch, my son Asa and I took off for a two-week adventure of a lifetime. Our good friend Daryl Roberts had invited us to join him in climbing Mount Kilimanjaro in Tanzania as part of a fundraising effort for Daryl's ministry, Orphan Aid Liberia. Daryl started the ministry back in 2008 when he witnessed firsthand how years of civil war and an Ebola outbreak had created tens of thousands of orphans in Liberia. Our family had supported Daryl's ministry for years. When he talked to me about climbing Kilimanjaro, I was hesitant because of my work and family obligations. But then I thought about taking Asa with me. The trip fell in the middle of Asa's senior year of high school, which was an odd time to take him out of school for two weeks. However, I knew from my experience with my three daughters that once he moved off to college, we'd probably never have an opportunity like this again.

Asa and I spent a year planning and dreaming about the trip. In addition to the hike up Kilimanjaro, we scheduled a safari in Ngorongoro Crater, one of the best places for safari on the entire African continent. As we counted down the days to our leaving, Asa and I could talk about nothing else. We were both incredibly excited.

But then the Melton case hit a crucial point, which made it nearly impossible for me to leave. I had just deposed Ebram Handy, one of GM's primary field performance engineers. Basically, when a GM product had a problem like the Cobalt ignition switch, Handy came in to investigate. I grilled Handy about the ignition switch, while Harold Franklin objected to my line of questioning from start to finish. Right after that came the motion-to-compel hearing, which we won. GM obeyed the judge's order and delivered the documents we needed. Doreen and I had just started going through them when it was time for me to go on my adventure with Asa. Everything going on at work told me to cancel the trip.

I left anyway.

Asa, Daryl, and I had the time of our lives. That's not to say climbing Kilimanjaro was easy. Far from it. We climbed the Lemosho route, which allowed us to climb the scenic western approach to the mountain. Unlike what you would think of a typical mountain climb, climbing Kilimanjaro means long treks each day up and then down as we made our way around the mountain. We had a number of porters who carried up much of the gear and food. They set up our tents before we arrived exhausted in camp each evening. Asa and I slept in the same tent each evening, which to me was the best part of the trip. We had many meaningful conversations, along with lighthearted banter back and forth. As much as I enjoyed the adventure of climbing, I found myself looking forward to the evenings with Asa.

Asa made me proud during the climbs each day. As Daryl and I struggled, Asa climbed like a mountain goat. In fact, our main guide gave him the nickname "Little Simba," in part because of his red hair but also because of his determined attitude.

My days weren't all fun, though. I called Doreen by satellite phone every evening for an update on the case. It was at a crucial point. Even though I had left the country for two weeks, I could not completely disengage.

During one call in the middle of our climb, Doreen picked up the line and immediately said, "You need to call Mark Hood."

"Why?" I asked.

"Just call him," she said. "He found something. You need to hear it from him."

I was puzzled, but I dialed Mark's number. He picked up.

"Lance, I figured out why the new Cobalt switch we tested had twice the tension as the one out of Brooke's car. GM changed it. They gave it a longer detent plunger and spring," Mark said.

I thought back to my deposition of Ebram Handy on February 1. I asked him point blank if the replacement switch for an '05 Cobalt was the same switch that originally came in the car. He talked around the question, saying something about how the specifications had not changed and how from a GM perspective they had not made a change as far as torque was concerned. When I pointed out that he had not answered my question, Harold Franklin objected and Handy refused to answer. I also asked Handy if any changes had been made to the '08 Cobalt switch to make it less likely to turn inadvertently from run to accessory. He assured me nothing had been changed. Now we had proof that he was lying.

"How did you figure it out?" I asked.

"I used everything I had to scan this thing every which way—electron microscope, computer tomography, stereomicroscope. That's how I first saw it. Then I took some switches apart. All the ones out of '05s and '06s have a shorter detent plunger. In the new ones, the plunger is just under a tenth of an inch longer, 0.082 inches to be exact. Nothing else is different. The diameter of the plunger and the size of the detent indentions are all the same. They just gave it a longer plunger and spring and the problem was fixed."

"The longer plunger and spring made that much difference?" I asked.

"Absolutely. I even tested the torque on an '05 switch, then replaced the plunger and spring with one out of a new switch. When I retested it, the torque had doubled," Mark said.

"So the lower torque numbers have nothing to do with wear and tear over time," I said.

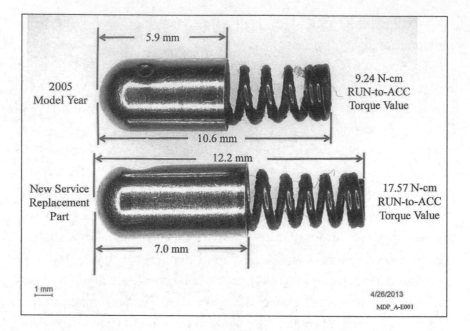

5.9 mm

2005
Model Year

9.24 N-cm
RUN-to-ACC
Torque Value

10.6 mm

12.2 mm

New Service
Replacement
Part

17.57 N-cm
RUN-to-ACC
Torque Value

7.0 mm

1 mm

4/26/2013

MDP_A-E001

"Not at all, because the numbers are consistent. The '05s and '06s and some of the '07s I test all come in around 11, 12 Newton centimeters of torque, with some even lower. The new ones all consistently measure 20 or more. When I measure the detent plungers, the older cars all measure the same, and the new ones all measure 0.082 inches longer," he said.

I thanked Mark for his hard work in uncovering the difference in the switches. Like Charlie Miller, Mark Hood went far beyond what we'd contracted with him to do. Once again, God brought the right people at just the right time to uncover what GM had tried to keep under wraps for a very long time.

Although I knew Mark's finding was another huge breakthrough, I also had a climb to finish. The last day and a half of climb and ascent was the most physically demanding activity I've ever engaged in. Asa, Daryl, and I arrived at the camp where we would start the ascent to the Uhuru Peak, Africa's highest point. Asa befriended a sixty-year-old woman during this time in the camp before we made our ascent to the peak. She had recently lost her husband. They had planned to climb Kilimanjaro together, and she still wanted to make it to the peak.

We set out on our ascent at 11:00 at night. Our guide wanted us to arrive at the Uhuru Peak just before sunrise. As we began to climb, it was pitch black. Our headlamps provided the only light to see where to climb. We then climbed. And climbed. And climbed. And climbed. Three hours later at 2:00 a.m., I was exhausted. When I looked up, all I saw was the headlamps of each climber in front of me in a line that looked like it went on for miles. Asa, on the other hand, lived up to the reputation he had gained on the mountain. He stayed right behind the guide the whole climb.

During the climb, we passed a number of people who were either resting or decided they could go no farther. We passed the sixty-year-old woman. Asa and I looked at her as we passed by. She was plodding along so slowly that we were both certain she would never make it to the top. Asa wanted to help her, but I told him she had a guide with her and there was nothing more we could do.

By 4:00 a.m., I had decided I wanted to quit. Asa kept me going. By 5:00 a.m., we could barely see the peak. Unfortunately, I was so light-headed and sick, I wasn't sure if I could keep going. As Daryl and I struggled up to the peak, Asa was there waiting for us. We reached the summit just as the sun began to rise over the Kenyan plains. The light bounced off the mountain's massive glaciers, creating a sight words cannot describe. Basking in the glory of God's creation with my oldest son truly was a spiritual experience. Right then I would not trade the experience for anything. Unfortunately, we were only allowed to remain at the peak for thirty minutes because of the risk of altitude sickness. As we began to prepare for our climb down, I heard Asa exclaim, "She made it!" I then looked to where Asa was pointing and saw the sixty-year-old woman trudging slowly up to the peak. The scene brought tears to my eyes. It still does.

Back at It

My trip with Asa was amazing, but I didn't have much time to reflect on it once I returned home. We'd scheduled Mark Hood's deposition the week after I got back.

Before I left, the timing seemed unfortunate but still manageable. Not anymore. If Harold asked Mark about the switch before I had a chance to question GM's people about the change, GM would have time to concoct some story that could explain away why a part changed but not the part number. Mark could not lie or hide what he'd found, not if asked directly about it. I could not take the chance of giving GM time to come up with a cover story. Ebram Handy evaded the question when I asked him, "When you buy a switch now, for example, like this from AC Delco for the '05—for a replacement for the '05 Cobalt—is this the same ignition switch as came with the Melton vehicle?" He answered by telling me the part number had not changed. I pressed and asked if the switch itself was the same. He replied, "Our specifications have not changed, so from a GM perspective, we have not made a change as far as the torque is concerned." In light of what Mark discovered, Handy's reply certainly implied he knew the switch had changed. I could not let them know that we had uncovered the truth.

I called Harold and told him I'd like to push Mark Hood's deposition back until after I had a chance to depose Ray DeGiorgio and Gary Altman. "I'd like for Mark to have their testimony in the event that he may have to rely upon it to support his opinion," I explained, which was true. Fortunately, Harold agreed. We pushed Mark's deposition back to mid-May while DeGiorgio and Altman were scheduled for May 1. Once again, the subject of mediating the case came up. As before, I told Harold I'd talk to my clients about it and get back to him.

Settling the case was the last thing on my mind now. We'd found so much, I could not help but think we were on the verge of uncovering even more.

And we were right.

Doreen and I began reviewing the documents GM produced in response to Judge Tanksley's order. We soon realized they were even more devastating for GM than the documents previously produced. In 2010, GM began a Cobalt airbag nondeploy investigation. Of course, this proved what we had suspected all along: there were documents about the ignition switch after 2009. The documents revealed GM knew of numerous crashes where airbags in Cobalts failed to deploy. They began the investigation purportedly to determine why this was happening, even though it was clear why. Keys were rotating to the accessory or off position during accidents, engines were shutting off, and Cobalt airbags were not deploying. It was plain as day. Instead of fixing the problem, GM fiddled around with more meetings and investigations in 2010, 2011, and 2012, which never resulted in any concrete actions being taken. In the meantime, GM customers were dying.

We learned this when we discovered a spreadsheet buried in the middle of the tens of thousands of documents GM produced. Two seemingly innocuous pages numbered by GM, documents 37916 and 37917. There were last names, car models, crash dates, and crash locations:

Rose, 2005 Cobalt, 7/29/2005, Marbury, MD
Culbert, 2005 Cobalt, 11/17/2005, Baldwin, LA
Carroll, 2005 Cobalt, 2/10/2006, Lenexa, VA
Oakley, 2005 Cobalt, 3//2006, Frederick, MD
Frei, 2005 Cobalt, 12/29/2006, Cellarville, PA
White, 2005 Cobalt, 2/6/2007, Shaler Township, PA
McCormick, 2006 Cobalt, 8/6/2007, Crosslanes, WV
Gathe, 2007 Cobalt, 9/26/2007, New Orleans, LA
Breen, 2005 Cobalt, 0/6/2007, Lyndhurst, OH
Register, 2006 Cobalt, 3/5/2007, Chattahoochee, FL
Freeman, 2006 Cobalt, 4/5/2008, Sommerville, TN

Wild, 2007 G5, 5/21/2008, Argyle, WI

McDonald, 2007 Cobalt, 5/29/2008, Lufkin, TX

Harding, 2006 Cobalt, 9/13/2008, Lincoln Township, MI

Dunn, 2008 Cobalt, 11/29/2008, Rolling Hills Estates, CA

Grondona, 2007 Cobalt, 12/6/2008, Lake Placid, FL

Lambert, 2005 Cobalt, 12/13/2009, Highland County, VA

Chansuthus, 2006 Cobalt, 12/31/2009, Rutherford County, TN

Najera, 2006 Cobalt, 12/31/2010, Harlingen, TX

Sullivan, 2007 Cobalt, 12/13/2011, Parksville, SC

Stover, 2005 Cobalt, 2/20/2011, Stokes, OH

Preuss, 2005 Cobalt, 8/12/2012, Mundelein, IL

Then it hit us. These were some of the victims GM had known about as far back as 2005. And likely there were many more.

There was also a cryptic reference to another crash in the spreadsheet. Instead of a last name, it said SCI IN—06-033, 2005 Cobalt, October 1, 2006, WI. This was the Rademaker crash. The fact that GM listed the special crash investigation number, as well as the date and location, definitively proved GM and its in-house lawyers knew about this one years before Brooke's crash.

The spreadsheet gave only last names and did not describe the injuries suffered in these accidents. I later learned "Rose" referred to Amber Rose, a sixteen-year-old girl who died on July 29, 2005, when her Cobalt airbags did not deploy in a crash because her key had also moved to the accessory position. Shortly after, Amber's mom, Terri DiBattista, hired a lawyer to investigate why the airbags had not deployed. GM's lawyers convinced Ms. DiBattista and her lawyer to enter into a confidential settlement. Many of the other names on this spreadsheet were also the drivers and passengers in Cobalts who died when their airbags did not deploy. GM convinced many of the families of the victims on the spreadsheet to confidentially settle their claims as well. These secret settlements enabled GM to withhold the damning evidence of what it knew about the ignition switch defect.

This cover-up was not limited to GM and its in-house lawyers. "Chansuthus" on the spreadsheet referred to Haysaya Chansuthus, a twenty-five-year-old nursing student who died of blunt brain trauma when her Cobalt went off the road and hit a tree. Haysaya was wearing her seat belt and the Cobalt's airbags did not deploy. The SDM showed her Cobalt's power mode status was in the off position. Another crash where the weak ignition switch caused the key to turn and the airbags not to deploy. In 2010, the Chansuthus family filed a lawsuit against GM. GM then hired King and Spalding, particularly Phil Holladay and Harold Franklin, to represent the company.

In 2010, Harold Franklin submitted his evaluation of the Chansuthus claim to GM's in-house lawyers. Harold warned GM it faced a significant punitive damages verdict due to the malfunction in the Cobalt preventing the airbags from deploying in a frontal impact. Of course, we did not file the Melton complaint until 2011. Subsequent disclosures revealed that Phil and Harold knew of other Cobalt ignition switch cases in addition to Chansuthus. They knew all along and were complicit in covering up these other crashes and fatalities until Judge Tanksley forced GM to disclose them.

We also later learned that the Lambert case on the spreadsheet involved Tonya Lambert, a thirty-five-year-old, who was seated in the right front passenger seat of a 2005 Cobalt on December 13, 2009. She was severely injured when the ignition switch in the Cobalt inadvertently turned off and caused her airbags not to deploy. She sued GM. As a result, GM's in-house lawyers met to discuss the case. One young attorney who had been with GM for only a few months asked why they had not issued a recall. He was quickly told engineering was "looking into it" and the lawyers had "done everything they could do." He was not to pursue this matter further. Meanwhile, GM and its lawyers repeatedly told me and the Meltons that they knew of no similar incidents involving Cobalts.

I also decided I wanted to depose Ray DeGiorgio as soon as possible. Not only did he design the Cobalt ignition switch, but his name continually came up in the Cobalt airbag nondeploy investigation documents. DeGiorgio and Altman played a large role in the November 2004 PRTS report. According to the report, Altman went to DeGiorgio asking for possible solutions to the low torque problem. DeGiorgio told him it would be nearly impossible to solve the problem without compromising the electronics within the switch. Later, Brian Stouffer, the leader of the Red X team, which exists to solve technical problems, asked DeGiorgio what it might cost to redesign the switch. DeGiorgio responded that his SWAG (silly wild-assed guess) was some outrageous number.

DeGiorgio's cavalier attitude, and his fellow employees' acceptance of it, disgusted me. From what I could surmise from the documents we'd received, DeGiorgio seemed to be responsible both for the low torque switch and for its remaining that way even after problems were discovered as far back as 2004. If anyone knew why the detent plunger suddenly grew by 0.082 inches, it had to be him. I couldn't wait to ask him about it.

With all the new developments, I had Ken and Beth come in to bring them up to date on everything. When I told them that we'd discovered GM had secretly changed the switch, Ken became emotional. "I knew it wasn't Brooke. I knew it wasn't Brooke," he repeated.

"No, it wasn't," I reassured him. "The switch was bad and their secretly changing it without changing the part number basically admits that. The part was bad. It needed to be changed, and they tried to do so quietly hoping no one would notice."

I paused for a moment before I broke the next set of news to them. Finally I said, "We've also learned that Brooke wasn't the only one to die."

Beth put her hand to her mouth. "Oh no. How many others have there been?"

"At least two dozen. The first was only sixteen when she died a month before Brooke even bought her car," I said.

Ken became visibly angry at this news.

Beth then asked the obvious question. "Shouldn't we contact someone in the government to try to force a recall?"

I wrestled with that question myself, not only when Beth asked but in the years since. When I talk about this case, many people have come up to me and asked why we didn't go public in some way as soon as we discovered the problem. My answer to Beth and my answer to those who ask now goes back to my days as a young, hotshot lawyer who was going to change the world. In the second chapter I mentioned a client I represented whose husband had died when a tire blew out and his Ford Bronco II rolled over. In the immediate years that followed, I represented a number of families in Bronco II cases.

Ford used the federal government in support of its defense. In 1989, NHTSA opened an investigation into the rollovers of the Bronco IIs. The administrator of NHTSA was Ralph Curry, a political appointee of President Bush. Curry involved himself in NHTSA's Bronco II investigation and influenced the decision to close the investigation in 1990 without finding a safety defect. Curry then left NHTSA and began being paid handsomely by Ford to testify that, since the federal government found the Bronco II was not defective, how could a jury find it was defective? I found myself fighting not only Ford but also the federal government when representing these families in Bronco II cases. The more I investigated, the more I learned that NHTSA was, and is, significantly influenced by car manufacturers. The reason is simple: money. NHTSA officials often go easy on car manufacturers hoping that they may be able to reap the rewards when transitioning to the private sector. Simply put, over the last forty years, there has been a "revolving door" where NHTSA employees work for a time, then leave to work for the industry. This incentivizes NHTSA officials to support the industry rather than consumers when it comes to automotive safety issues. You cannot bite the hand you are hoping will feed you.

I told this story to Ken and Beth. "You'd think that it would make sense to send what we've uncovered to NHTSA and they would force

GM to recall every vehicle with this switch in it, not just Cobalts but Saturns and everything else they put this into. But I think there's just as good a chance that the opposite would happen. NHTSA could whitewash this whole thing, and that would give GM ammunition to use in court just as Ford did with the Bronco IIs," I explained. "I can see contacting them only hurting our case. And it's not like NHTSA doesn't know people have died because of this switch. They knew about the sixteen-year-old girl who died in a Cobalt all the way back in 2005 or '06. They did nothing then. I can't see them doing anything more now."

More than my experience with the Bronco II case influenced my advice on this question. Over the course of my career, I've watched as those who work for government agencies charged with regulating different industries end up going to work for or lobbying on behalf of the very people over whom they were supposed to provide oversight on behalf of the American people. It's a revolving door that goes both ways regardless of whether the Democrats or Republicans are in office. The American people are left with watered down regulations and lax enforcement of the rules on the books. Only the civil justice system truly holds giant corporations like General Motors accountable. I did not want to risk the Cobalt becoming another Bronco II case by going to NHTSA at this stage.

The timing of our conversation also impacted my decision. Less than four years had passed since the federal government bailed General Motors Corporation out of bankruptcy by purchasing the company and having it reconstitute itself under the name General Motors LLC on July 1, 2009. In their very first response to our lawsuit, GM had tried to use this change as a way of dodging responsibility for any car manufactured by "old" GM. The deal cost taxpayers billions of dollars. GM could not now afford a massive recall and the financial hit they'd take, and the federal government would perhaps be hesitant to risk the billions they'd poured into the company as well. On top of that, the federal government had already shown a proclivity for going along with GM in their argument that a moving stall was not a safety issue. Did that decision have something to do with the bailout? I couldn't help but wonder. Even if it didn't, I had no faith that the government agency that had already received reports of deaths caused by the defective switch in the Cobalt and deemed it not to be a safety issue would now change their minds because another young woman had died.

Before Ken and Beth left, I had to discuss one more issue with them. "Harold Franklin has asked again if you would be willing to enter into mediation and settle this case now." Even before the words were out of my mouth, I could sense neither of them was in any mood to consider settling.

"You know, Lance, we've always deferred to your judgment on this, and we will this time as well," Ken said.

"The clock is ticking on GM, not us. I see no reason whatsoever to mediate now. Doreen is still working through the 20,000 documents they last sent us, and we have more depositions scheduled, including one with the man who designed the ignition switch," I said.

"I wish I could be there and look across the table at him and ask him why he let something he knew didn't work go into our daughter's car," Ken said. "I want to look him in the eye and ask him that."

"That's not possible now, but when we go to trial, you can be there when I get him on the stand and I ask him just that," I said.

"I can't wait," Ken said.

CHAPTER 11

Dropping the Bomb

"Have you done anything on your own since November of 2012 to look into why these keys in certain Cobalt vehicles turned from run to accessory under certain operating conditions?" I asked the lead design engineer of the Cobalt ignition switch, Ray DeGiorgio, during his April 29, 2013, deposition.

Two years had passed since I first filed the lawsuit for the Meltons. I'd spent most of that time waiting out GM's delay tactics and sorting through tens of thousands of pages of documents looking for something, anything, pertinent to our case. Through all of that digging, one name stood out, Ray DeGiorgio, the man behind this switch, and the man who vehemently maintained it was next to impossible to change its design in a manner that met GM's standard of "acceptable business practice." From the day I first saw his name, I wanted to have him answer questions under oath. That day was today.

Throughout the afternoon I'd asked questions establishing that he had designed the switch and signed off on approving it for use in not only the Cobalt but also the Saturn Ion, Pontiac G6, Pontiac Solstice, Saturn Sky, and Chevy HHR. He was the first in-house switch designer GM had used in a long time. Prior to this particular switch, outside suppliers both designed and manufactured all ignition switches used in General Motors products. Ironically, complaints about the shoddy quality of the outsourced switches brought the design process in-house, although Delphi continued manufacturing the switches DeGiorgio designed.

"No, I have not [looked into that]. Trying to get ahold of this hardware is not easy, as you probably know," DeGiorgio replied.

"Do you plan on doing anything more?"

"I do not have any plans at the moment."

"So as far as you're concerned, this matter is closed as far as the redesign?" I said. No matter what DeGiorgio said in reply, I knew I had him right where I wanted him, and this case along with him.

One of the senior partners at King and Spalding, and the head of their automotive and transportation division, Philip Holladay, represented GM at this deposition, having replaced Harold Franklin. Mr. Holladay's presence sent a clear message—GM was concerned that the Melton case was spinning out of control.

Holladay spoke up. "Object to form. You can answer."

"In order for me to pursue design changes regarding this switch, I would need the program team's approvals, and of course, all that requires resources, which I do not have," DeGiorgio said.

My heart skipped a beat when he said this. Rarely do witnesses recite the exact line you need to set them up to fall, but DeGiorgio just did. I'd taken my time with my questions to lead him to this point. Earlier DeGiorgio acknowledged a couple of incidents had occurred, which prompted GM to issue a service bulletin and offer complaining customers the option of a key with a hole rather than a slot. However, he proudly stated that the fact that hardly any customers took GM up on their offer confirmed that any problems were very, very rare. DeGiorgio also testified that even his own son drove a 2007 Cobalt. If that didn't speak of his confidence in this product, what did?

Not only was he confident of his switch, he made it very clear over the course of his testimony that the switch had never been changed, nor did it need to be, with two small exceptions. Not long after the release of the 2003 Saturn Ion, the first car to use this ignition switch, customers complained of difficulty turning it on during cold mornings. DeGiorgio looked into the problem and ordered a change in the grease inside the switch. When I asked if the torque-rotation curve remained the same even with the new grease, he replied, "The torque rotation better be the same." The other change came in 2008 when they added a theft resistor to the electronics of the switch. Beyond adding a new resistor, nothing else was touched.

We also discussed the different investigations into the low torque complaints and the possibility of redesigning the switch. He made it clear that he thought the problem was overblown and that the switch had never been changed. To do so would require a massive redesign, adding a second detent, at a cost of hundreds of thousands of dollars. That's why GM didn't touch the switch, he claimed. He had even taken some replacement switches apart, trying to find a reason for the difference in torque reported between the '05–'07 Cobalts and the '08s and later. After what he called a high-level type of visual inspection, he determined no changes had been made. And, given what I had just asked him, no changes would ever be made.

I then handed DeGiorgio a photograph. "Let me show you what I'll mark as Exhibit 12. Can you identify that for us, please?"

"This looks like the—I want to say the '08 Cobalt ignition switch," DeGiorgio replied.

After clarifying how he was certain the switch was from an '08 Cobalt, I said, "Let me show you what I'll mark as Exhibit 13 . . . and that is the cutout of a . . ."

Before I could finish, DeGiorgio said, "Detent plunger."

"Detent plunger for the Cobalt?" I finished.

"That looks like the detent plunger on the—yes, on the switch," DeGiorgio said.

"Okay. And I'll represent to you this is the detent plunger for the '05 or '06 Cobalt." Then I picked up another photograph. "Let me show you what I'll mark as Exhibit 14, which is the detent plunger for a—it's either an '08 Cobalt or a replacement switch. Can you hold those up for the jury, please?" I said. There was no jury present. We videotaped the deposition so that it could be shown in court in front of a jury at a later time.

DeGiorgio held up the two photographs.

"The one on the right, Exhibit 13, is an '05 or an '06," I continued, "and the one on the left, Exhibit 14, is either an '08 or replacement. Do you see the difference?" This was the kind of moment attorneys dream of, that Perry Mason/Matlock/any TV lawyer moment where you drop a bombshell in front of a witness you are certain knows far, far more than he lets on.

DeGiorgio sat there, silent, staring at the photographs for what felt like a very long time. I looked over at Phil Holladay as if to say, *He has to answer this.* Holladay did not move or say a word. Finally, DeGiorgio said simply, "Yes."

"Have you noticed that before today, Mr. DeGiorgio?"

Another long, uncomfortable pause followed before DeGiorgio lied and said, "No, sir."

"Were you aware of this before today, Mr. DeGiorgio?"

Exhibit 13 (left) and Exhibit 14

"Object to form," Phil Holladay said, then added, "You can answer."

"No, sir," DeGiorgio replied.

"It appears to be pretty clear that the plunger and the cap is taller on Exhibit 14 compared to Exhibit 13, isn't it?" I asked.

"That's correct," DeGiorgio admitted. At this point I was fortunate Ray DeGiorgio was answering these questions himself. He'd never given testimony in a deposition before, which means he was more candid than someone more experienced in these matters like Brian Everest. Rather than dance around my questions, he answered, and his answers were as much a bombshell for General Motors' defense in this case as any evidence I'd presented.

"How is a taller cap going to affect the rotational resistance?" I asked.

This was a question he seemed to want to answer. "It's hard to determine from these pictures exactly if it is a taller cap or if it is recessed inside the house or not. It's hard for me to assess, really, what I'm looking at," he said.

That answer struck me as absurd. "You've taken apart a number of switches and you're telling the jury you've never noticed the difference in the plunger between the '05 and '06 versus the new resistor or switch?" I asked.

I knew no one would believe that explanation. Phil Holladay knew it too. "Object to form," he said.

"I did not notice, no," DeGiorgio said.

Perhaps this would have been a good time to remind the witness that he was under oath, but I did not. Instead I fed him more rope with which to hang himself. "Let me show you what I will mark as Exhibit 15," I said, handing him a photograph. "Do you see this photograph, Mr. DeGiorgio?"

"Yes," he said.

"Can you hold that up for the jury, please?" I asked and he complied. "The plunger and spring on the '05 is up top and the replacement switch is down below. Do you see that?"

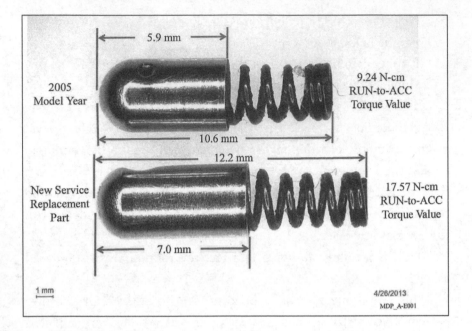

2005 Model Year — 5.9 mm — 10.6 mm — 9.24 N-cm RUN-to-ACC Torque Value

New Service Replacement Part — 12.2 mm — 7.0 mm — 17.57 N-cm RUN-to-ACC Torque Value

1 mm

4/26/2013

MDP_A-E001

"Object to form, lack of foundation," Holladay said, "but you can answer."

"Yes, I do," DeGiorgio said without elaborating. The plunger and spring on the top photo was clearly shorter than the one in the bottom photo, 0.082 inches to be exact.

"And I'll ask you the same question. You were not aware before today that GM had changed the spring—excuse me—the spring on the ignition switch had been changed from the '05 to the replacement switch?"

As if on cue, Holladay said, "Object to form. Lack of predicate and foundation. You can answer."

"I was not aware of a detent plunger switch change. We certainly did not approve a detent plunger design change," DeGiorgio said.

"Well, suppliers aren't supposed to make changes such as this without GM's approval, correct?" I asked. I had him on the ropes.

"That is correct."

"And are you saying that no one at GM, as far as you know, was aware of this before today?"

"Object. Lack of predicate and foundation. You can answer."

"I am not aware about this change," DeGiorgio said.

After then asking him if the change in detent plunger and spring could explain the high torque resistance numbers in the replacement switch (his response: "That's hard to assess"), I asked, "What do you intend to do with this information, Mr. DeGiorgio?"

Holladay objected before DeGiorgio said, "Quite frankly, I would have to go back and look at some of these parts if they changed."

"Don't you think you should do that?" I said.

"Yes."

"This would not have been an impossible change to make in 2005, would it?" I asked in direct reference both to his earlier testimony and to documents going back to the first PRTS where DeGiorgio claimed changing the switch would be next to impossible and very expensive.

"Object to form," Holladay said.

"Let me answer this question," DeGiorgio asserted. "Changing the spring or rate would require revalidation of the switch. Revalidation of the switch would mean you have to go through all the testing procedures that we had done previously. That's something that would need to be carried out with a new detent plunger."

"And you didn't want to do the revalidation, did you?" I fired back.

"Object to form."

"That's not correct. The revalidation would have been done by the supplier, not necessarily me. My point here is changing the spring would require a revalidation by the supplier for the new spring. That was never brought to my attention," DeGiorgio said.

"You were the one that was supposed to bring the design changes to the ignition switch to Mr.—what's his name—Sullaj's attention." Blendi Sullaj was DeGiorgio's immediate supervisor. "That was your job, wasn't it, back in 2005?"

"Object to form, you can answer."

"Your job was to bring potential solutions to Mr. Sullaj," I added.

"I did," DeGiorgio said.

"And one of the solutions could have been changing the design of the spring to the way it is in the replacement switch, correct?" I said, not letting up.

"Object to the form," Holladay said again.

"Again, changing the spring would require validation," DeGiorgio said, clinging to that phrase like a lifeline.

"Sure, but it wasn't impossible to do that, was it?" I fired back.

"You cannot—I cannot assess that because I don't know the results of changing the spring," DeGiorgio said.

"And you didn't do anything to assess that in 2005, is that correct?"

"I was asked to provide a solution or enhanced change to address a potential issue, and my design—my direction was to provide them with a new switch design," DeGiorgio said.

I didn't need to ask another question. Our case was made. DeGiorgio and the rest of his team found a simple solution to fixing the deadly low torque problem that allowed keys to turn from run to accessory, a solution they should have implemented before Brooke ever bought her car. They secretly changed the ignition switch, which made the new cars safer, but allowed millions of GM customers to continue to drive cars with the dangerously defective ignition switch. Changing the switch without changing the number and without recalling cars already on the road was the ultimate cover-up. DeGiorgio and everyone else who signed off on this change (and a change like this does not happen without being approved on up the chain of command) knew exactly what they were doing. They just hoped they'd never be found out, and now they were.

Phil Holladay realized what a disastrous development this was for GM's case. We later learned that during the deposition, Holladay emailed Ron Porter, the GM in-house attorney overseeing the Melton case, telling him that a bombshell had just been dropped. Porter then came by the Westin to pick up copies of the exhibits immediately after DeGiorgio's deposition. We also learned that from that point forward, Holladay began telling GM that they had to settle this case as soon as possible. He emphatically told them they did not want to go in front of a jury with the evidence we'd just dropped on Ray DeGiorgio.

Even worse for GM was the fact that DeGiorgio perjured himself with his answers. In layman's terms, he lied. Repeatedly. Even worse, DeGiorgio had an opportunity to fix his answers when he was given the opportunity to read through the transcript of his testimony. Every deposed witness in any civil case must sign a printed transcript of his or her testimony to affirm that their testimony is true and correct. The attorneys representing them must also sign off on it. If they misspoke, or outright lied, this gives them a chance to backtrack and tell the truth. DeGiorgio signed off under penalty of perjury without making a single change. It is one thing to get caught red-handed in a lie, but another to think about those lies for thirty days and then say everything was 100 percent true. Then someone from King and Spalding signed off as well, suborning his perjury. This point became very important on down the line, but that's for another chapter.

On June 12, 2013, just over six weeks after deposing Ray DeGiorgio, I flew back to Michigan to depose Gary Altman. Altman had served as the Cobalt program engineering manager, which means he essentially oversaw the development and launch of the Cobalt from design through engineering to manufacturing of the car. He also had the distinction of experiencing a moving stall in a Cobalt in the fall of 2004 on GM's Milford proving grounds track. Unlike most people who experienced a Cobalt turning itself off, Altman tried to make his car turn off by intentionally hitting the key fob with his knee while driving. He did this after a member of the press had his Cobalt stall right before the launch of the car line. He later left the Cobalt program in the summer of 2005 for another assignment within GM.

I decided on a different approach with Altman. I started his deposition with a questionnaire I'd prepared for the occasion. I handed a copy to Altman and read the first question on my list: "'The safety of consumers should be GM's number one priority.' Do you agree with that?" I asked.

"Agree," Altman said.

"So we'll mark that as 'yes,'" I said. "'GM should never put profits over the safety of consumers.' Do you agree with that?" I asked.

Harold Franklin had returned for this deposition rather than Phil Holladay. "Object to form," Harold spoke up.

"Agree," Altman said.

I went on down through my questionnaire to establish that GM should never sell a car it knows does not meet its minimum standards for safety, and that if it does, it has an obligation to warn consumers of that fact. Harold objected throughout while Altman answered each question in the affirmative. Then I brought the whole thing home with my tenth question: "The key in the 2005 Cobalt should not inadvertently move from run to accessory while driving the car."

"Object to form," Harold said.

"No, it should not," Altman said. Like Ray DeGiorgio, Gary Altman had never testified in a deposition before. An engineer, he was accustomed to giving direct answers. I appreciated his candor. I don't know that the opposing counsel did.

After filling out the questionnaire with Altman's answers, I then said, "What I'd like for you to do is sign the bottom of this second page, please."

Harold spoke up. "I'm going to object to—Lance, can you tell us where that came from?"

"I prepared this document. You can sign it," I said.

After Harold objected again, Altman stopped writing and refused to sign it on the advice of his counsel, although he'd already written his first name at the bottom of the page.

Now that I had established that Gary Altman believed GM had an obligation to produce a safe product, I dove into a line of questions designed to show the Cobalt was not safe. "Mr. Altman, the key's moving from the run to the accessory position in the 2005 Cobalt can be dangerous in certain situations, can't it?"

Harold objected before Altman said, "That answer would have a lot of qualifications to it." We discussed those qualifications. Altman maintained, as GM had all along, that a car can still be controlled after the engine shuts off and the driver loses power steering and brakes. After pressing on this matter for several questions, I moved on to the ignition switch. I showed Altman Exhibits 13, 14, and 15 from the DeGiorgio deposition. He told me he'd never seen them before.

Then I asked, "Were you aware before today that the ignition switch in the 2005 Cobalt did not meet GM's minimum torque performance requirements?"

Harold objected before Altman answered, "I don't recall that, no."

"And the vehicle never should have been sold if it didn't meet GM's minimum torque performance requirements, should it?"

Harold objected before Altman answered, "That's correct."

"And the reason is because that could be dangerous under certain conditions, because the key can move from run to accessory?"

Harold objected before Altman answered, "Yes."

I could have stopped there because this was an earth-shattering admission from a senior GM engineer, the man who was over the entire Cobalt project. Under oath he clearly said that this car never should have been sold with an ignition switch that failed to meet GM's own torque requirements. But I wasn't finished.

For the next several minutes I went through all the "fixes" GM engineers had come up with for the Cobalt, as well as the fixes they dismissed because they did not meet acceptable business practices. I hoped to show that, at the very least, Brooke Melton should have received a different key when she bought her Cobalt. Both Charlie Miller and Mark Hood had told me that if her key had a hole rather than a slot, in all likelihood her car never would have shut off and she would be alive today. As we turned up the heat on GM, their legal team and witnesses tried to pass the blame on to Thornton Chevrolet for not finding the service bulletin about inadvertent engine shutoffs when she brought her car in for service. The point I wanted to make, and did make, was that GM knew about this problem before Brooke ever bought her car. They had an obligation to change the key before she bought the car, not after she had a problem with it.

That line of questioning led to the final point I wanted to make. I took Altman to a GM document titled "Winning with Integrity, Our Values and Guidelines for Employee Conduct." I opened it to the second page, third paragraph, and read, "Our steadfast commitment to doing the right thing to achieve our business objectives through personal responsibility and accountability." I then asked, "Now, GM did not do the right thing when it came to Brooke Melton's Cobalt, did it?"

"Object to form," Harold said, but I was undeterred.

Before Altman could answer, I fired another question. "It should have sold her a Cobalt where the key would not move from run to accessory if she inadvertently hit the key, shouldn't they?" I felt like I was back in my days playing college football. I knew I had him on the ropes. Now it was time to keep pounding away until he broke.

Altman stammered and said, "I would say that, again, we didn't have an alternative solution that would guarantee that could not happen."

"Well, if you didn't have a solution, you just should have at least told her, shouldn't you?" I said, keeping the pressure high.

"Object to form," Harold said.

"She should have known about this problem, shouldn't she?" I said, leaning in.

"Object to form," Harold said.

Altman had a deer-in-the-headlights look to him and the car was bearing down. "It's difficult to answer that one because there are many things in the vehicle that way," he said. "If something inadvertently is actuated, there could be consequences, yes."

"Under what circumstances should GM have not told Brooke Melton about this problem with her vehicle before she bought it?" Altman was an engineer. I knew he thought in terms of solving problems, and he had a huge one in front of him right now.

"Object to form. Lack of foundation," Harold said right on cue.

"There are many other things in a vehicle that have the same consequences if they're improperly used, they're improperly actuated," Altman said without answering my question.

"So is it your position as the program engineering manager for the 2005 Cobalt that it was okay for GM not to tell Brooke Melton about this problem with her vehicle before she bought it?" I fired back.

"I was not," Altman said before Harold interrupted with another objection, "the program engineering manager at that time. I was—back in March of '05 is when I started to leave the program. I was gone by May of '05. I was not there at the time when this service fix and everything got completely out in the field and completed." If he thought this let him off the hook, he was mistaken.

"So if you were the program engineering manager at the time, you think she should have been told, correct?" I said. I could not wait for his answer.

"Object to form. Calls for speculation," Harold said, trying to create a safe space for his client not to answer the question. It did not work.

"I think the insert should have been put into the car, yes," Altman said.

"Her car?" I asked.

"As a," Altman continued, only to have Harold object in the middle of his statement, "containment issue."

"No further questions. Thank you, sir," I said.

I didn't need to ask anything else. Gary Altman, the man responsible for bringing the Cobalt from an idea to fruition, just admitted that GM should have warned Brooke of the defect in her car before she bought it, and should have provided the "fix" they'd come up with to deal with the problem rather than trying to pretend there was no problem. As soon as he admitted that, it was time to drop the mic. Boom. Altman's testimony on top of DeGiorgio's meant one thing for General Motors: the jig was up.

I felt like I'd just broke open for an eighty-yard touchdown run with less than a minute to go on the clock. However, as certain as I was that the combination of DeGiorgio and Altman's testimonies was a game-over moment for GM, they still had the chance to throw a Hail Mary. They designed, manufactured, and installed an ignition switch that did not meet their minimum safety requirements. When confronted with this fact, they not only covered it up but changed the part and pretended it had never changed. However, as I cautioned Ken and Beth shortly after Altman's deposition, GM had issued a technical service bulletin and that gave them a possible out. They could still claim they had identified the answer and provided a possible fix, yet Thornton Chevrolet failed to locate the TSM or make the necessary repairs. I had them dead to rights on the switch cover-up, but GM still had some cards to play.

CHAPTER 12

The End?

In the wake of the DeGiorgio and Altman depositions, I felt very good about where the Melton case stood. We had the kind of evidence that doesn't just sway a jury but makes them angry. That was my goal because I myself was angry over all our team had uncovered. When I stood before a jury, I wanted them to share my outrage.

However, even with the evidence and the testimony we'd collected thus far, I knew winning this case was not a slam dunk. The jury might, in fact, be incensed over GM's negligence, but that did not guarantee a verdict in our favor. I'd lost too many cases when the evidence clearly leaned in my favor to feel comfortable now.

Both Charlie Miller and Mark Hood had told me that if the Thornton Chevrolet service technician who worked on Brooke's car had read the service bulletin and replaced her slotted key with a hole, her car never would have gone from run to accessory, which means she never would have lost control and lost her life. Yes, GM had acted negligently, even recklessly. They should have ordered a recall when they first found the problem and, at the very least, fixed the keys. Once they figured out that changing the length of the detent plunger and spring could fix the low torque problem, they should have issued a recall and changed the ignition switch in every Cobalt already on the road. Yes, GM should have done all those things, yet there was a chance that the jury could still find in their favor, because if Thornton Chevrolet had taken the prescribed action from the GM service bulletin, the Melton accident would not have happened.

This tension created an interesting dynamic through this phase of the discovery process. Not only did I depose GM witnesses, I also deposed key people from Thornton in November 2012 and April 2013. While General Motors' legal team never went after Thornton themselves, they sat back during the depositions and let me do the damage for them. When I asked Thornton's people pointed questions about why the service department did not check for the service bulletin related to moving stalls (although it did not use the word "stall"), GM's attorneys didn't come to Thornton's defense, but they also did not pile on with more questions about why they didn't do more. Instead GM's attorneys were happy to allow us to make our case against Thornton. In the end, our casting blame on the dealership helped GM's defense.

Thornton's attorneys took a similar approach to GM. To them, the more we showed GM acted recklessly and was negligent, the less likely we were to come after them. To their credit, everyone we deposed from Thornton was quick to accept responsibility for their actions without excuse. Their attorneys, however, used the defense that GM should have done more. GM discovered the problem with the switch long before Brooke Melton bought her car, and many years before she ever brought it in to them for service, they argued. At the very least, GM should have changed the key when Brooke's Cobalt rolled off the assembly line rather than wait for customers to have a problem before they took action. And while GM had issued a service bulletin, they did so in December 2005 and October 2006. How reasonable is it to expect a mechanic to sort through more than two hundred service bulletins to find one that is several years old for every car that comes into the shop for repair? Yes, Thornton's service department should have done more, their attorneys essentially argued, but what they should have done paled in comparison to GM's misconduct. They were, therefore, content to sit back and let us go after GM, confident that a jury would find the carmaker's actions so egregious that any judgment against the dealership would be quite small.

I thought they both should be held accountable. The actions of one in no way nullified or lessened the responsibility of the other. Every step we took in this case came out of this conviction. I looked forward to making my case against each one before a jury.

By the summer of 2013, GM made it very clear they did not want to see this case go to trial. They pressed me to convince my clients to consider mediation. Only later did I learn that Philip Holladay appeared before a May 15, 2013, GM roundtable which had met to discuss our case. He told the collection of attorneys and executives that I would have little problem convincing most jurors that the Cobalt ignition switch was substandard and defective, and that GM had known about the flaws with the product since the first Cobalt rolled off the assembly line. Yet GM had done essentially nothing about it. If this case went all the way to trial, GM would lose and suffer a "substantial adverse verdict."[4] "This case has to be settled," he argued.

I wasn't quite ready to settle. I continued deposing key GM people throughout the spring and early summer. From March through June 2013, we also filed three more requests for documents. I requested all the documents related to similar cases as well as any documents related to the switch changes that seemingly no one in all of GM knew anything about. I knew there had to be a paper trail. There always is in companies like this. DeGiorgio himself testified that any change to any part in any GM car undergoes thorough testing. Design changes must also be communicated with schematics and engineering drawings to the company that makes the part, in this case Delphi. All of this creates a paper trail and requires many people to sign off approving the change. This could not have been the work of a single rogue employee, as GM later tried to claim. If it were, GM needed to admit it under penalty of perjury. I requested that GM state they did not request and were not asked to authorize or approve a change in the cap and spring in the ignition switch. I wanted their denial on the record.

In response to our requests, GM sent us nearly 100,000 pages of warranty claims, most of which were useless in terms of finding any pertinent information. Names and places were, again, conspicuously absent. Judge Tanksley in her ruling on our motion to compel ordered General Motors to produce all responsive documents related to that investigation. GM refused to comply in violation of the court order. It also instructed its employees not to answer questions during depositions about these documents, citing a self-critical analysis privilege. A 2007 ruling made it clear that there is no such law under Georgia law. Even so, GM hid behind it to keep from producing what we needed.

Fighting GM to force them to do what a court had already ordered them to do grew wearying. On June 18, 2013, I filed a motion for sanctions. As part of the sanctions, I requested that the court force GM to pay all our expenses caused by their refusal to obey the earlier court order, including paying attorneys' fees and expenses for filing the motion. For more than two years, they'd tried to stonewall and delay us into submission. We, however, continued to plug along. Although it would have been easy to get frustrated, and admittedly at times it was, I did my best to remain focused on the goal of taking them before a jury.

"We need to settle this."

As the fight for compliance continued, Harold continued making it clear that GM wanted to settle the case. In late summer 2013, he called and told me that mediation with us had been discussed at the highest levels at GM. "They are willing to do what it takes to settle this," he told me.

As with all the previous overtures, I told Harold I'd talk with Ken and Beth and get back with him.

"I hope they'll listen to you," Harold said. "I know you feel you're in prime position with this case, but keep in mind that at the end of the day, Thornton Chevrolet had a chance to make the necessary repairs that would have prevented this tragedy from ever happening."

"I think there's a lot of blame to go around," I replied, "but I know your client is very serious about settling and we will give it thoughtful consideration."

When Ken and Beth and I sat down to discuss GM's latest attempt at mediation, I told them it may be time to at least listen. "I think GM is about to do everything they can to shift blame to the dealership. While I don't think a jury will buy it, you never know. There is the chance that when all is said and done, GM will find a way to wriggle off the hook. It won't hurt to at least sit down and hear what they have to say," I said.

"What about a recall?" Ken asked.

"We can't make that a condition for settling," I said. "Something like that goes beyond the scope of our lawsuit. Like we talked about before, NHTSA should have already been all over this, but they've chosen to do nothing. I'm not sure that will change. However, if we settle with GM, we'll still have a trial with Thornton, and that gives us a chance to make all we've found public."

"So you think we should hear what they have to say?" Ken asked.

"I do," I said.

Ken and Beth looked at one another. This wasn't our first conversation about mediation, which meant they had clearly discussed it together before. "Lance, throughout this whole thing we've trusted your judgment. There's no need to change now. If you think we should hear them out, then let's do it," Ken said.

"We really just want to put this whole thing behind us," Beth said. "We have the answers we wanted. We know this wasn't Brooke's fault, and hopefully we've done enough to keep this from happening again."

"Okay," I said, "I'll make the call."

Later I called Harold and told him we were ready to hear what they had to offer. "Great," he said. "We'll get everything set up and go from there."

On August 23, 2013, the Meltons and I went to mediator Victor Faenza's office in Atlanta. Both Harold Franklin and Phil Holladay were there along with Trish Jankowski who came down from Detroit to represent GM. Thornton Chevrolet's insurance's attorney, Shawn Kalfus, represented them. They, too, wanted to discuss a settlement with us. All of us met together in a large conference room where all parties made their case. Victor then explained the mediation process and what he hoped to accomplish that day. Normally, I, as the lawyer for the Meltons, would state the merits of our case and the lawyers for GM and Thornton would respond. I told Victor, however, we could dispense with this posturing and get down to the business at hand: determining whether GM and Thornton were willing to do the right thing.

We stayed in the conference room while the GM and Thornton lawyers and reps went to separate rooms. Since we had made a demand on both GM and Thornton, Victor met with each of them to obtain their initial offers. As the mediator, Victor had one goal: to settle the case. Mediators are known by their "success rate."

Victor's task was not easy. The mediation process can strike those new to it as morbid and wrong. In a way, the mediator tries to put a value on a life that has been lost. Not all lives are valued the same. For example, a young father or mother who makes $100,000 a year who dies and leaves behind a spouse and three children is viewed differently than a single man at thirty who dies childless. The former has a lifetime of earnings that are taken into consideration, and while the latter leaves a huge void, there's not a financial blow others suffer as a result of his passing. However, our case was not the norm. This was not only about placing a value on Brooke's life but also about punishing GM for its egregious misconduct. That's why I asked for $8 million. Georgia law allows for consideration of essentially a penalty on the company for their negligence, rather than simply considering the case as some sort of retroactive life insurance policy.

Ken and Beth and I took our place in the room assigned to us and waited. And waited. And waited. Finally the mediator came in and said, "We have a joint offer. GM and Thornton together have offered to settle for $250,000."

"Apiece?" Ken asked.

"No, total, together," the mediator said.

At that Ken started to explode, but I stepped in and defused the situation. "Listen," I said, "we're about to walk out. We are not going to sit here all day and go back and forth with such ridiculous offers. I thought they were serious about settling, but obviously that is not the case."

"So you are rejecting the offer?" the mediator asked.

"Absolutely," I said.

"Do you want to counter?" he asked.

"Same number as before," I said. "Eight million."

"Okay. I will be back with their responses," he said.

A few minutes later the mediator returned. "General Motors is very serious about settling this case today, but the dealership is not interested in that. Would you like to speak with GM separately?" he asked.

I briefly consulted with Ken and Beth, then said, "Yes."

Once the mediator left, I told Ken and Beth that we could still proceed with the case against the dealership even if we settled with General Motors. "We'll still take this to trial," I said. "In a way this is even better for us. When we go to trial with Thornton, we can bring out all the evidence we have of how GM kept all this hidden for so long. Even though we'll have to sign a confidentiality agreement with GM, they won't be able to keep this under wraps any longer." The Meltons liked that idea.

A while later the mediator returned with another offer from GM. While it was higher than the previous offer, it still fell well below what we needed not to take this to trial. I had discussed this process with Ken and Beth before we arrived. The day wore on and GM was still nowhere close to it. Finally I told the mediator, "Listen, we're tired of this back-and-forth. If they want to settle, they are going to have to pay my clients five million dollars. That's it. No negotiation. Five million or we're done."

"Okay. I will tell them," he said.

A short time later he returned and said, "The representatives from GM do not have the authority to authorize that size of an agreement today."

"I don't care if they have it or not," I said, tired from what felt like a wasted day. "It's five million or we'll see them in court."

The mediator took my message to the other side. When he returned, he asked if I could keep this offer open for the next twenty-four hours. I agreed.

My phone rang first thing the next morning. It was Phil Holladay. "We'll pay the five," he said. Frankly, I was surprised. "Of course there will be a confidentiality agreement they will need to sign," he said.

"Of course," I replied.

"And we will need all the documents we produced to be returned to us," he said.

"No, that won't be possible," I said.

My reply took Holladay by surprise. "Now you know that's pretty standard procedure in cases like this, Lance. We produced those for you in good faith. Once the case settles, you no longer have claim to them. You will need to return them and delete any electronic copies you may have."

I was ready for that. Ken and Beth and I had discussed this scenario. More than anything, they wanted the truth about what GM had hidden for so long to come out. We could not do that with the confidentiality agreement. However, in a trial against Thornton Chevrolet, we could prove that Thornton certainly should have done more when Brooke brought her car in for service of the moving stall, and in the process, we could expose GM's role.

"But the case isn't over," I said to Phil Holladay. "We still face a trial with the dealership next month. All of these documents are key to our case against them. Since the dealership didn't want to settle, we can't turn loose of anything until that trial is over and done with."

"But Lance . . ." Holladay said. The two of us went back and forth for a while. Allowing us to keep such damning documents after sign-ing a confidentiality agreement was very much out of the ordinary. That's part of the reason for settling. Companies go through mediation and settle cases to keep all of the negative evidence against them out of the public domain. But I was not about to relent. The only way we'd settle was if we kept the documents and received payment of five million dollars. In the end, Holladay said, "Okay. Deal."

I called Ken and Beth as soon as I hung up with Holladay. "It's over," I said. "GM agreed to pay the five million and to allow us to keep the documents for the trial against Thornton."

"So we won?" Ken said, almost in shock.

"We did," I said. It was a very emotional moment for both of us. After I hung up the phone, I sank down in my chair and let out a long sigh. I thought about how close I came to not taking this case and about how so many factors had to come together at just the right time for this victory to have been possible.

And yet at the same time, I could not help but think this could not be the end. How many more Ken and Beth Meltons were out there, grieving family members who needlessly lost a child or a husband or a wife because of GM's negligence? We knew of at least two dozen other crashes with fatalities and injuries. Many of these crashes resulted in lawsuits which were settled quietly with the plaintiffs agreeing to confidentiality agreements as part of their settlements. Silence and secrecy led to more people dying. The more I thought about it, the more I knew I needed to act. This case wasn't just about justice for Brooke Melton and her family. This was about justice, period. Now I just had to figure out what my next course of action should be.

CHAPTER 13

All Out in the Open

In early February 2014, five months after we settled with GM, Sean Kane called me with some big news. "Lance, GM just issued a recall on the ignition switch in the Cobalt."

"What? How did they finally come around to doing that?" I asked.

"I don't know when they made the actual decision, but with all their layers of bureaucracy, it took until now for them finally to announce it," Sean said.

"And in the meantime?" I asked.

"I am sure there have been accidents, and probably more fatalities, between the time you showed them the defect last spring and now," Sean said. "And it gets worse," he added.

"Worse?! How could it possibly get any worse?" I said.

"Their letter to NHTSA and the recall notice don't say a word about any deaths. Nor does it in any way indicate they've known about this problem for a decade. The wording makes it sound like they just discovered this minor little defect that they decided they should probably do something about before someone gets hurt. I quote, 'If the key is not in the run position, the airbags may not deploy if the vehicle is involved in a crash, increasing the risk of injury.' They also limited the recall to '05 through '07 Cobalts and their Pontiac twin, the G5."

I was livid. "That's it? That switch is in a lot more cars than that!"

"I know," Sean said.

"And GM conveniently forgot to mention that when the key turns off, you lose your power steering and every safety system, and the transmission may do a hard downshift that can cause you to lose control of your car." I had to pause before I totally lost control. "So how many vehicles did they actually recall?"

"Just over 600,000," Sean said with a sarcastic laugh.

"So what can we do?" I asked.

"I have a couple of ideas," Sean said.

Over the next couple of hours, Sean and I plotted out a strategy to get the word out that the defective switch affected more than the Cobalt and G5. However, I had to be very careful because of the confidentiality agreement I'd signed with GM. I still had options, beginning with the government agency in charge of regulating the auto industry.

Every car recall goes through NHTSA first. Now that they were involved, I could go directly to them with some of the information I had attained through the course of the lawsuit in order to demonstrate to them that this safety defect went beyond the scope of GM's limited recall. With Sean's help, I drafted a Notice of Inquiry letter to NHTSA in which I made it clear that GM had known about this ignition switch problem for at least a decade. Under federal law, General Motors, like every other manufacturer doing business in the United States, must report any safety defect to NHTSA within five days of its discovery. Again, the confidentiality agreement prevented me from telling the feds everything I knew, but I was able to share enough to put NHTSA on notice that this problem went back farther and impacted far more vehicles than GM had let on.

I wish I could say that sending this letter to NHTSA solved the problem. In a perfect world, alerting the agency who sets the rules for automotive recalls should have brought the weight of the federal government down upon GM and forced them to expand the recall in the interest of saving lives. Of course, in that perfect world, NHTSA would have acted when it received 260 complaints over eleven years of cars suddenly turning themselves off, but in the world in which we live, they did not. Contacting NHTSA was a necessary step, but I knew GM needed more pressure before they'd do the right thing. And nothing puts pressure on a public entity like bad press.

Through his work on safety issues, Sean had formed many relationships with people in media outlets that cover the car industry. After we drafted the letter to NHTSA, Sean said, "I have a friend named Jim Healey at *USA Today* that I think would be interested in this story. I think we need to contact him."

At first I protested. I told Sean I could not go to the press because that would put the Meltons' settlement with GM at risk. We couldn't sign a piece of paper saying we wouldn't talk about the terms of the settlement or the details of the suit and then turn around a few months later and do just that. Yet the more we talked, the more I knew I needed to do this. Granted, it might put me at risk of GM coming after me, but that was a chance worth taking.

I called Ken and Beth first to let them know what I was doing. I did not ask their permission, nor did I consult with them to see if they wanted to be a part of my talking to the press. Either such action could put them at risk of violating the confidentiality agreement and thus losing their settlement. This action was purely my own. If GM came after anyone, it would be me and me alone. Having said that, Ken and Beth were both happy that I could finally expose this problem. Before the recall, our hands were tied. But now, since GM had "self-reported," I had the freedom to go to NHTSA and tell them that GM had not told them everything. And since the recall was in the news, I had the freedom to comment on it as well.

I then contacted Jim Healey. The two of us talked at length about the Melton case and the Cobalt. In the course of our conversation, I was careful not to reveal direct testimony, nor did I produce any documents for him. Instead, I recited facts in a more general sense, along with citing sources he could look up on his own and verify, such as the articles written at the time of the Cobalt's release.

A couple of days later, my phone rang. "Hey, son," my dad said, "I'm sitting here in a Waffle House, reading the paper, and I thought you might want to know that you are on the front page of the *USA Today* business section." He was right. I did want to know that.

I went out and found a copy of the paper. When I opened to the business section, I found this headline above the fold: "Lawyer asks feds to force GM to explain recall timing." The article included this quote from my letter to NHTSA, which was also my shot across the bow of GM letting them know that we weren't going to let them continue to sweep this under the rug. "Testimony of GM engineers and documents produced in *Melton v. General Motors et al.* show that the automaker actually knew about the defective ignition switch in these vehicles in 2004 before it began selling the 2005 Chevrolet Cobalt."

But this was only one of two stories by Jim Healey about the Cobalt recall in the February 19, 2014, edition of *USA Today*. The second had the headline: "Lawsuit: GM knew of Cobalt ignition problem." Its first paragraph went right to the point: "General Motors knew in 2004, a decade before it issued a recall, that its Chevrolet Cobalt had an ignition switch that could inadvertently shut off the engine while driving, according to depositions in a civil lawsuit against GM. The stall also would cut off the driver's power steering and brakes, as well as safety systems such as airbags and antilock brakes."

The story went on to expose the basics of the case against GM, explaining how they knew about the problem from the day one of their engineers experienced a moving stall while testing a Cobalt prior to its release, yet did not correct the problem. When customers complained, they came up with a snap-on cover for the key, which changed the slot to a hole. Healey quoted Gary Altman calling this an improvement but not a fix. Yet they did not install the insert on new cars before they were sold, which Altman said they should have. The story also gave details of Brooke's fatal accident, making sure to include the fact that this happened on her twenty-ninth birthday.

Healey closed the article by explaining how the "black box dump" (the SDM data readout) revealed the ignition key had moved out of run and shut off the engine at the time of the crash. "Cooper argues that is what caused Melton to lose control," was the last line of the article.

After I finished reading the two articles, all I could think was, *Well, here we go.* I didn't know if Harold or someone from GM's legal team might call and threaten to pull the settlement, or if perhaps NHTSA might contact me and ask for more information. I never heard from either because the story immediately blew up beyond *USA Today*.

The day after Jim Healey's story ran, the *CBS Evening News* featured an investigative report of their own into the Cobalt ignition switch. Their report focused on the accident Sean Kane uncovered more than a year before during our search for other fatal crashes: Amy Rademaker and Natasha Weigel. Watching Jeff Glor's interview with both girls' grieving parents, I became angry all over again. The report quoted my letter to NHTSA, which made it clear GM knew about this problem years before these two teenagers were killed and did nothing about it.

As part of the report, Glor also interviewed former NHTSA head, Joan Claybrook. "This is an immoral act by General Motors to cover up this defect," she said, "not to tell people and then the result was inevitable, that people were going to die and be injured and that to me is unconscionable. *It's like throwing an airplane passenger out without a parachute*" (emphasis added). I couldn't have said it better myself.

The *CBS News* report ended with Amy's mother, Margie Beskau, looking into the camera and saying, "It made me angry. They knew something was wrong with the car before the accident. I just don't understand how they can knowingly put these cars out and still let people drive them. This is my child. This is my baby girl."

After that, every major news outlet was all over the GM ignition switch story. My phone rang off the hook with calls from reporters and news stations across the country. As satisfying as it was finally to see the truth plastered across headlines, I couldn't help but wish that none of this was necessary. That's one of the most frustrating parts of my job. As rewarding as it is to hold companies accountable and force them to do the right thing, I always wish they had just done the right thing in the first place.

On February 25, GM expanded the recall to an additional 748,024 vehicles, including the 2006–2007 Chevrolet HHR and Pontiac Solstice, along with the 2003–2007 Saturn Ion and the 2007 Saturn Sky. In their letter to NHTSA explaining the reasons, GM did not mention Sean's and my letter to NHTSA or the negative stories that topped the headlines every day thanks to us. Instead GM worded the recall notification in a way that implied that in the course of their due diligence and commitment to safety, they uncovered more vehicles that might be at risk.

The expanded recall did nothing to slow the feeding frenzy that was now underway. More stories came out every day from other media outlets, all talking about how GM had hidden a deadly secret for a decade. GM acknowledged half a dozen deaths, which made report-ers dig even deeper to find out how many people had actually died as a result of the Cobalt switch. Personal injury lawyers pounced as well. Television commercials sprang up overnight promising to get you money if you'd been hurt in a GM vehicle because of the faulty ignition switch. Thousands of lawsuits were filed against GM over the next couple of months.

I didn't advertise, but my office was inundated with calls as well from both prospective clients and attorneys across the country with GM ignition switch claims. As I wrote in the beginning of this book, my office is small and I like it that way. Most years I take on no more than fifteen or twenty new clients. In early 2014 I could have taken on as many as my heart desired, hundreds if I had wanted. One attor-ney about whom I will write much more later took on more than a thousand GM ignition switch cases. We would come to learn that the majority of those cases had zero merit, but that didn't stop him and others from signing up people left and right. Blood was in the water and the sharks were swarming. I had no interest in doing business that way, but I did want to help those who called my office with legitimate claims. I just didn't have the staff, or the time, to help them all.

A solution presented itself when two fellow attorneys and friends from a Montgomery, Alabama, firm with a national reach asked me to meet them for lunch. Cole Portis and Gibson Vance had both worked for the firm of Beasley Allen for years, but more important, they both shared a strong Christian faith and deep convictions about doing their work with integrity. Over lunch they got right to the point. "Lance," Cole said, "we are overrun with GM ignition switch cases, but you are the man who knows and understands this better than any other attorney in the country."

"I get calls about them every day myself, more than I can handle," I said.

"We get that and we don't want to put more on your plate. But here's what we'd like to do. We'd like to partner with you on these cases. We have the resources to handle them, and you have the expertise," Gibson said.

The idea sounded good to me. We spent the next hour talking over details, then shook hands to seal the deal. No contracts were ever drawn up and signed. We didn't need them. Over the next couple of months, we selected around a hundred cases we all felt good about representing. In the process we probably turned down five times that amount. Some of those we turned down did not have merit, but others simply lacked the kind of hard evidence we'd need to make their claim. The last thing we wanted to do was get people's hopes up and then have to turn around several months or a year later and tell them that there was nothing more we could do for them.

In the meantime, GM's recall kept growing, with a little help, I might add. I filed a pleading in California as part of a class action suit in which I was involved. In the pleading I pointed out that many more GM cars should be recalled. Coincidentally, at least according to GM, on March 27, 2014, they expanded the recall to include the 2008–2010 model years of the Cobalt, Sky, G5, and Solstice and the 2008–2011 HHR. Altogether, the recall now included 2,190,934 vehicles. The number grew to 2.6 million a month later. On June 30, GM recalled an additional 8.4 million vehicles for defective switches. These did not share the same switch as the Cobalt. Problem ignition switches went across all boundaries at GM. They weren't finished yet. By the end of 2014, GM had recalled nearly 30.1 million cars, trucks, and SUVs for a variety of reasons, but most related to faulty ignition switches.

The ever expanding recalls were only the beginning. In early March, NHTSA demanded GM turn over all documents related to the ignition switch problem. At long last they wanted to know what GM knew about the switch, when they knew it, and why they had not notified NHTSA earlier. The United States Justice Department launched its own criminal investigation. Federal prosecutors in New York began exploring the question of whether GM misled federal regulators as to the extent of the problem on top of their failure to comply with federal law requiring they disclose safety defects within five days of discovery. That opened the door for charges to be filed against individuals, with the very real possibility that someone could go to jail.

And then Congress got involved.

Senator Jay Rockefeller of West Virginia asked Senator Claire McCaskill to have the Senate Commerce, Science, and Transportation Subcommittee on Consumer Protection, Product Safety, and Insurance hold hearings, which she did. A House committee also launched its own investigation. Both demanded copies of all of GM's records related to the faulty switches. Hearings in both the House and Senate were scheduled as early as April. Witnesses were subpoenaed. Senators and members of Congress wanted to know why a company the United States had rescued from going under had willfully covered up the fact that their product killed people, and that they knew about the deaths and did nothing to prevent them nor recall the defective product as soon as they learned there was a problem.

Watching all this unfold, I could not have been happier. From the start, this was the result we wanted. I never wanted this case drawn out to the point of having the head of GM dragged before Congress to answer once and for all why GM had covered up this problem. Honestly, all I ever really wanted was for them to acknowledge the full extent of the problem and then fix it before anyone else died. The fact that they waited more than two months between deciding to issue a recall and then finally doing it set me off. There was no accountability here, no taking of responsibility. Instead, it was the same old GM, hiding problems until they had no choice but to act. And that's what the press and all the investigations finally did; they left GM no choice but finally to do the right thing. Their new CEO, Mary Barra, said they acted out of the new GM's commitment to quality and the safety of their customers. If that were true, it wouldn't have taken them so long to issue a recall, nor would they have rolled out the recall in spurts. Yes, I felt quite satisfied that what was hidden was now out in the light. And now that it was all out in the open, I hoped those behind the cover-up would finally be held responsible for their actions.

With all of this coming less than five years after bankruptcy, GM found itself reeling. Commentators began asking if this might be the final blow for the beleaguered company that would put them out of business. Sales of GM cars dropped, while the resale value of the affected vehicles plummeted. Clearly, GM had to do something to try to get out in front of this story before the company did indeed go under.

CHAPTER 14

Finally Accountable?

Throughout the three-year ordeal of our lawsuit against GM, Ken and Beth Melton made it clear that they just wanted the truth to come out so that other families would not have to experience what they had gone through. Brooke's death was horrible and so unnecessary. If their tragedy could somehow prevent another death, her parents could find some degree of comfort in that. That's part of what made GM's lines of defense so infuriating.

Throughout the process of our lawsuit, GM claimed they were in no way responsible for Brooke's death. In the beginning, they maintained, even though eyewitnesses said it was barely sprinkling at the time of the accident, that Brooke died because she decided to drive too fast on a rain-slick highway. Then GM pointed the finger at a faulty alarm system Brooke chose to put in her car. Even when it became clear the ignition switch was the cause of the accident, they deflected blame. Brooke had too many keys on her key chain or she had her seat too close to the dashboard, they said. At one time GM even implied that perhaps Brooke panicked when her car started to skid, and she turned her car off herself while traveling 58 mph down the highway.

Whatever the cause, from GM's perspective, the fault for the accident all came back to a poor decision Brooke made. There was nothing redemptive about her death, nothing in it that could serve a greater good except perhaps the timeless lesson to make better choices. And while GM's decision to settle the case for an unprecedented amount might have felt to our side like an admission of their guilt, GM's silence in the aftermath and the limited nature of the first recall on February 7, 2014, showed they felt otherwise.

That is why I felt somewhat vindicated when the April 2, 2014, Senate Commerce, Science, and Transportation Subcommittee on Consumer Protection, Product Safety, and Insurance hearing on the GM ignition switch recall opened with Subcommittee Chair Claire McCaskill of Missouri reading these words:

> It was a rainy night. On March 10th, 2010, Brooke Melton, who was twenty-nine years old and a pediatric nurse, was driving her 2005 Chevy Cobalt to meet her boyfriend for her birthday dinner outside of Atlanta. As she was driving on the highway, her car suddenly lost power. Unable to control the vehicle, it hydroplaned, crossed the center line, and slammed into another vehicle at 58 miles per hour. Her car ended up in a creek. The airbags never deployed.
>
> Ken and Beth Melton, her parents, rushed to the hospital, but she was dead when they arrived. In their nightmare of grief, they hired a lawyer, a trial lawyer. They asked him to help them understand what had happened, and if possible, hold whoever was responsible accountable. And he went to work, spending his own resources to get to the bottom of what happened to Brooke on that rainy night in Georgia when she was on her way to celebrate her birthday.
>
> He hired an engineer to help him. Together, Mr. Cooper, the lawyer, and Mr. Hood, an engineer, began to identify a defect that someone at General Motors had discovered years before. There was a problem with the ignition switch in Chevy Cobalts. It could easily be bumped or brushed or pulled from "on" to "accessory" or "off," powering down the car, disabling the power steering, disabling the power brakes, and preventing the airbag from deploying.

After two years of fighting General Motors for documents and a timeline of events, at a deposition in April of last year, Mr. Cooper finally confronted General Motors with the facts. Someone at General Motors had switched out the unsafe ignition switches in several car models and covered it up by using the same part number for the same switch—for the new switch—had covered it up by using the same part number for the new switch . . .

. . . Further, it is now clear that GM knew of the faulty switch in 2004, knew the airbags were not deploying in 2005, and in late 2005, knew someone had died. We don't know how many people crashed because of this cover-up. We do know that many died, including Ms. Melton and at least one of my constituents, a Missouri woman who died in a crash in 2009 in the suburbs surrounding St. Louis . . .

. . . It might have been the old GM that started sweeping this defect under the rug ten years ago, but even under the new GM, the company waited nine months to take action after being confronted with specific evidence of this egregious violation of public trust.

Senator McCaskill wasn't just reading this statement for the other members of the subcommittee or for those watching at home. Her words were primarily directed at the witness sitting directly in front of her, the chief executive officer of General Motors Corporation, Mary Barra. Senator McCaskill concluded her opening remarks by saying, "It's time that we finally get this right so that it doesn't take an enterprising trial lawyer and an engineer that he hired to bring to light what NHTSA should have known long ago, and what General Motors should have fixed long before Ken and Beth Melton lost their daughter Brooke."

Watching at home on television, I could not help but think that these words were a gift to Ken and Beth. Their daughter's tragic, needless, completely preventable death now had a larger meaning. Because of her, and because of her parents' unceasing quest for the answer to what really happened on the night of her death, General Motors was now being held accountable for their actions by none other than the United States Congress. I had spoken with Senator McCaskill before the hearings and filled her in on many of the details that she included in her statement and also used when questioning Mary Barra. I got emotional watching. This moment was the real payoff that told me all we went through with this case was worth it. Mary Barra was now being confronted directly by Brooke's story, and the stories of other people who died because of this ignition switch. Perhaps a few naïve souls expected Ms. Barra to come clean in this hearing about everything GM knew and when they knew it. I was not one of them. Even so, watching her squirm in front of a panel of senators gave me a great deal of satisfaction.

April Fool's Day in the House

Ms. Barra had the chance for transparency on April 1 when she spoke before a House subcommittee at a hearing titled "The GM Ignition Switch Recall: Why Did It Take So Long?" She didn't take it. Instead she announced that she had asked former US Attorney Anton Valukas to conduct a "thorough and unimpeded" investigation into the Cobalt switch issue as well as the overall culture of General Motors during that time. "He has the free rein to go where the facts take him, regardless of the outcome. The facts will be the facts," she declared. "Once they are in, my leadership team and I will do what's necessary to assure this doesn't happen again. We will hold ourselves accountable."

Her answers over the course of the House hearing made it clear that accountability did not include the congressional hearings.

Immediately after Barra read her opening statement to the House subcommittee, the chairman, Representative Timothy Murphy of Pennsylvania, directed her attention to an email between two GM employees where one said the Cobalt was blowing up in their faces, and it was just being bumped by the driver's knee. Barra replied with what was going to become the answer of the day: "Clearly there were a lot of things that happened. There's been a lot of statements made as it relates. That's why we've hired Anton Valukas to do a complete investigation of this process. We are spanning over a decade of time."

Representative Murphy immediately asked, "But you don't know why they didn't just replace the switch on the old cars as well as the new cars?"

"I do not know the answer to that, and that's why we're doing this investigation," Barra calmly replied.

"Given the number of complaints about ignitions turning off while driving, why wasn't this identified as a safety issue?" Representative Murphy asked.

"Again, I can't answer specific questions about that point in time. That's why we're doing a full and complete investigation."

Representative Murphy did not give up his quest to get a direct answer. "Let me—another one. In the chronology GM submitted to NHTSA, GM states it didn't make the connection between the ignition switch problems and the airbag nondeployment problems till late 2013. So my question is, when GM decided to switch the ignition in 2006, did the company ever examine how a faulty ignition switch could affect other vehicle systems like the airbags?"

I knew what Ms. Barra was going to say before Representative Murphy even finished his question. Predictably she said, "Again, that's part of the investigation."

That exchange set the tone for every other round of questions directed toward Barra. Not only did she hide behind the "that's part of the investigation" line, she also invoked the old GM/new GM distinction that GM's legal team used in their initial response to our lawsuit. She repeatedly spoke of "today's GM," which values the customer as its compass along with relationships and individual excellence. The old GM was only about containing costs and maximizing profits. The new GM puts quality and the needs of the customer over all else. Barra referenced the investigation so often, along with references to the new GM, that *Saturday Night Live* parodied it four days later as the show's cold open.

To the Senate

After watching the House hearing on April 1, I expected more of the same the next day when Barra appeared before the Senate. I was not disappointed. Senator McCaskill opened the questioning by asking, "In April and May of last year, GM's employees were deposed in the lawsuit trying to get some kind of justice for Brooke Melton. They were confronted in the deposition with the fact that there were two different parts with the same part number and the different torque on both of those parts leading to the malfunction of the ignition switch. At that deposition, General Motors had a lawyer, and it was very clear at that deposition that there were two parts with the same number and that they had been switched out and that one of them was defective. When that lawyer for General Motors left that hearing, who did he report to?"

"I don't know which lawyer was at that trial, so I can't answer that question," Barra replied.

"Well, hold on and I'll get it for you," Senator McCaskill said. "You have some lawyers with you today, don't you? Don't you have your general counsel with you?"

"Yes, I do."

"You're free to confer with him if he would like to tell you who that lawyer would report to after that deposition," Senator McCaskill said.

Rather than turn and ask her counsel that question, Barra replied, "Again, we are doing a full investigation with Mr. Valukas, and all of the individuals that are associated with this incident will be a part of that, and the findings will be conclusive."

As this line of questioning continued, McCaskill later asked, "So, what I want to know is, what investigation began after that deposition?"

"That is part of the investigation," Barra replied.

I laughed out loud at the absurdity of her statement. Mary Barra was not there to answer questions but to deflect all blame and responsibility on whomever the Valukas report singled out. Nor did she plan to acknowledge any role the Melton lawsuit or my actions may have played in the ever-expanding recall. Senator McCaskill asked Barra directly about this. The senator pointed out that twelve days after the limited recall was announced, I wrote a letter to NHTSA explaining how the recall was not complete. Six days later GM expanded the recall. Senator McCaskill went on to say that I had filed another court pleading saying there were additional defective cars, and four days later, GM issued a third round of recalls. Senator McCaskill then asked, "Is this the new GM, Ms. Barra? Is this the new GM that takes a lawyer having to write NHTSA, and a court pleading for you to finally recall all the cars that had been impacted by this defective switch?"

Barra replied, "As we looked at the first population of vehicles, we immediately go and then read across to the other vehicles that may have the same part. Often, when you have the same part in another vehicle, it can be a different configuration, a different geometry. As we looked into that population, we then recalled that population, and then we immediately started to look up where were the spare parts," and on and on and on.

In other words, the timing was all coincidental.

The senators on the panel became visibly frustrated by Barra's lack of answers. Senator Dean Heller of Nevada started off skeptical that the hearing was going to produce much of anything. In his opening remarks, he said, "It is possible that GM has an explanation for why it took so long to pull these cars off the road. However, after yesterday's hearing, I'm afraid we're not going to get too many answers today."

California senator Barbara Boxer, however, kept pressing. She wanted to learn at the very least when Mary Barra, who had been CEO for only three months but had worked for GM for three decades, first became aware of the ignition switch problem. Boxer asked, "I have here a timeline of when the company knew there were problems.

It starts in '01. In '03, a service technician of GM noted that there was a stall while driving. And it goes on, and there's a constant theme here of the thing that's getting worse and worse through the years. Now, you're new at your job, but you've been at GM for how many years?"

"Thirty-three," Barra answered.

"Thirty-three years. So, when this was first discovered, you were executive director of competitive operations engineering, where you developed and executed strategies to improve the effectiveness of vehicle manufacturing and engineering, but you didn't know of this?" Boxer asked.

"Correct," Barra replied.

"Nobody told you about this?" Boxer asked, incredulous.

"Correct."

"Okay. And then you were plant manager of Detroit-Hamtramck Assembly in '03 to '04, where you were responsible for day-to-day plant activities related to safety, people, and quality, and still, you knew nothing about this?"

"We didn't build any of these models at the Detroit-Hamtramck plant," Barra said.

"In that position, you knew nothing about this, correct?" Boxer fired back.

"Correct," Barra replied.

"Okay. And then, in '04 to '05, you were executive director, manufacturing engineering, responsible for developing and implementing global bills of process and equipment to optimize capital deployment and manufacturing operating costs, and you developed and continuously improved lean cost initiatives. You knew nothing about this when you were executive director of manufacturing and engineering?" Boxer continued.

"Correct."

"You knew nothing? How about when you were vice president of global manufacturing engineering, '08 to '09? You knew nothing?" Boxer asked.

"Correct," Barra said again.

"And still you knew nothing when you were vice president of global human resources?"

"Correct."

Senator Boxer then said what I and everyone else watching this hearing of the Senate Commerce, Science, and Transportation Subcommittee on Consumer Protection, Product Safety, and Insurance had to be thinking: "You're a really important person to this company. Something is very strange that such a top employee would know nothing."

Later in the hearing, after other senators had asked question after question, most of which were answered with some variation of "That's why we are investigating" or "I don't know," Boxer blurted out in frustration, "You don't know anything about anything."

Game Changer

I felt a variety of emotions while watching this hearing on television. I felt gratified for the way the members of the committee honored Brooke and the others who had died as a result of this ignition switch. At times I became angry at how callous Ms. Barra seemed as she danced around questions rather than answering them directly. I laughed out loud at some of the more absurd portions of her testimony and at some of the senators' reactions to her. But I was never surprised, not by her deferring any probing question to the upcoming Valukas investigation, nor by her denials when asked about what she should have known long before January 31, 2014, which she claimed was the first time she ever heard about the Cobalt ignition switch problems, nor by anything else until . . .

Toward the end of the hearing, Senator McCaskill asked a question to which I also wanted an answer: "Ms. Barra, how many lawsuits relating to the defect both pending and closed, as well as settlements, has GM been a defendant or codefendant?"

"I don't have that information. I can provide it to the committee," Barra replied.

"I'm assuming you've had some briefings from your counsel about your exposure on this defect?"

"We have not talked about exposure. We're—we have—it's very important once we realized the situation, we immediately hired Anton Valukas. We don't want to have multiple investigations. We thought it was most important to have . . ."

Senator McCaskill cut her off. "I'm not talking about investigations. I'm saying as the CEO of General Motors, you have not had a briefing by your general counsel about the litigation that is ongoing against your company concerning this defect. You've not had that conversation?"

"I've been focused on getting parts for the customers," Barra said, as if she were personally running around from warehouse to warehouse trying to secure enough replacement switches for all two and a half million cars that had thus far been recalled.

One thing Barra had not yet done was actually answer the question. That fact was not lost on Senator McCaskill. The senator fired back, "We would like to know how many cases have been filed. We would like to know how many cases have been completed. We would like to know how many are settled. And most important, how many of those required confidentiality? How much whack-a-mole has been going on in terms of trying to deal with these lawsuits on a one-off basis, and leveraging what a lawyer wants to do for their client with the requirement of secrecy?" And then she added, "Has Mr. DeGiorgio been fired?" My ears perked up. I had wondered that myself.

"The investigation has been going on for only a couple of weeks. We have already made process steps. As I return to the office, we will start to look at the people implications," Barra said.

"So he has not been fired?"

"No, he has not."

"Okay. Is he still working there every day?"

"Yes."

"Okay. And you know that he lied under oath," Senator McCaskill said. Now she had my full and undivided attention.

"The data that's been put in front of me indicates that, but I'm waiting for the full investigation. I want to be fair," Barra replied.

I knew DeGiorgio lied when he said he knew nothing about the changes to the ignition switch, but I did not have any data to prove it. I wanted to know what data had been placed in front of the CEO of GM that showed he was lying. That same data should have been produced to Judge Tanksley's court when Harold claimed that General Motors had produced everything for us.

"Okay. Well, let me help you here," Senator McCaskill said. "He said several times he had no idea these changes had been made. Here is a document that he signed under his name, Mr. Ray DeGiorgio; he signed it on April 26th, 2006, approving of the change."

I sat there stunned but not fully surprised. For months I demanded this very document. Judge Tanksley had also ordered GM to produce any and every document related to the change in the switch, but over and over we were told no such document existed. And now, right in front of me on C-SPAN's coverage of the Senate subcommittee hearing, Senator Claire McCaskill had the very document in her hand.

It was as though Senator McCaskill could read my mind. She then asked, "Now, here's a really important question. This document, which is completely relevant to any lawsuit that is filed against GM around these crashes, would have been included in any document request from any lawyer representing a family. This document was not given to Mr. Cooper. This document was withheld from the lawyer representing the family of Brooke Melton . . . How do you justify withholding a key piece of documentary evidence in a litigation concerning a part that was changed without a part number change, as it is spelled out in this document for anyone to read? How does that happen?"

"I cannot—I don't condone not providing information when requested in a legal proceeding," Barra stammered. "And if that was done, we will deal with the individuals accountable for that."

There was no question of *if* that was done. Senator McCaskill was holding the very document GM had denied even existed. I wondered how many other key pieces of evidence GM did not produce over the past three years. I knew Sean Kane was closely following these hearings, so I called him. He had connections with several representatives and senators. I asked him to find out if GM had produced any other documents they had withheld from us. Earlier in the hearing, Senator Kelly Ann Ayotte of New Hampshire had said that GM's changing the ignition switch without changing the part number went beyond unacceptable. She said she believed it was criminal. In light of what I had just seen in these hearings, I was certain that wasn't the only criminal act committed by GM. Since I had already settled my case, there really wasn't anything I could do about it. At least there shouldn't have been.

CHAPTER 15

Back On

"I'm praying about doing something that doesn't make a lot of sense, but I think it is something I need to do," I said to Sonja the evening after Mary Barra testified before the Senate subcommittee.

My patient wife gave me that "I'm not sure where this is going" look and asked, "What is it?"

I took a deep breath. Honestly, I didn't know if I could force the words that were forming in my brain out of my mouth. It had not been that long ago I'd lost three major cases in a row, leaving my firm $2 million in debt and our house on the verge of foreclosure. What I was contemplating was not, in the words of General Motors, "an acceptable business case," but the more I prayed about it, the more strongly I felt it was something I had to do.

"Come on, Lance. Tell me, what are you thinking about doing?" Sonja asked again.

"Well," I said, then took another deep breath, "I am seriously considering recommending to Ken and Beth that we rescind the GM settlement and refile the lawsuit."

"Which means . . ."

"Which means we return the five million to GM, including all of the money that covered my expenses and fees." I had a little trouble believing I'd just said what I'd said. The crazy thing was, it made perfect sense once I said it out loud.

"So talk me through it," Sonja said.

"Well, in official legal terms, I'm pissed off," I said.

Sonja laughed. "Really?" she said with a sarcastic tinge. "I hadn't noticed."

"Yeah, I feel like GM pulled one over on us," I said. "It looks like we settled with them under completely false pretenses. They lied to us, Sonja. Harold and Phil Holladay and everyone at King and Spalding. Or maybe GM lied to them too. I don't know. All I know is Judge Tanksley ordered them to produce documents, and they lied to her and us and said the documents we wanted didn't exist. Then I saw Claire McCaskill holding one of these nonexistent documents. *The* nonexistent document that if I'd had, I never would have settled. I would have forced them into court and made them air out every piece of their dirty laundry for all the world to see."

"Yeah, I can understand why you are mad. I would be too," Sonja said. She paused for a moment before adding, "But rescinding the settlement, that's—that's huge."

"I know. Believe me, I know. The good thing is if I rescind, I can refile the case back in Judge Tanksley's court. They didn't just lie to us; GM lied to her as well. I can scream about that all day now, and no one will care because the case is settled. But if I rescind and refile, then the game changes once again. It may not be a completely civil action any longer. DeGiorgio, he lied under oath. GM and King and Spalding were complicit. That makes this fraud," I said.

Sonja let out a long sigh. "What do you think Ken and Beth will say? They've been through so much already. Can you really drag them back into the middle of this after telling them it was over?"

I shook my head and said, "I don't know. That's what I'm praying about."

A few days later I set up a meeting with Ken and Beth to explain what was on my mind. "Let me tell you what I'm thinking," I said when they came into my office. "GM lied to us before we settled. They lied about what documents they had on the change in the switch and they withheld documents regarding other lawsuits and settlements that are out there. They committed fraud. Not only did they lie to us, they lied to Judge Tanksley."

"How might these other documents have changed your mind about the settlement we accepted?" Beth asked.

"If we'd had these documents, we would not have settled when we did. And they can't hide behind their 'old GM' mantra on this one. This was the new GM that withheld documents but then went before the court and said they'd produced everything. I'm curious what else they've hidden from us and what it will mean for our case. I'm thinking . . ." I paused. "I'm thinking we should rescind the settlement and refile the case."

"Okay," Ken said.

"But . . . but under Georgia law, if we rescind a settlement, we have to offer to give the money back," I said.

"We've spent some of it," Beth confessed.

"I know. And this doesn't just apply to you. It will mean I give back all of my fees as well, but I am willing to do that." I thought for a moment to choose just the right words. "This is—this is a very serious decision. It's a risky decision too. Just because we refile doesn't mean we will automatically win the case. There's a chance we may not, the same chance that made me recommend we settle before. Why don't you go home and talk this over and then we will meet again in a few days and make a decision?"

Ken and Beth looked at one another and then Ken spoke up. "We don't need to go home to talk this over. If this is what you feel is the right thing to do, we'll do it. We've trusted you all along so far. We trust you here."

"I appreciate that," I said, "but we probably need to talk this through a little more and make sure we are all on the same page and that we are comfortable with where this might go. This isn't going to be like last time. Before, no one knew or cared that we'd filed suit against GM. But now the press is going to be all over this. When we refile, you are basically jumping into the fire and it's going to be hotter than ever."

"Listen, Lance, if you feel like this is the best way to do this because they haven't told us everything, then we are with you," Ken said.

Beth spoke up. "I do have one question. Why can't another lawyer do this? Why can't they file for someone else and ask for these same documents?"

"That's a really good question, and the answer is they really can't. The key here is Judge Tanksley. She had already ordered them to produce documents and they turned around and lied to her and said they had given us everything when they hadn't. When we get before her, she is not going to be happy with them, to say the least."

"Okay. That's good enough for me," Beth said.

"Me too," Ken said.

"All right," I said. "Well, that's what we'll do then."

A Deal's a Deal

The next day, April 11, 2014, I sent a certified letter to Phil Holladay officially rescinding the settlement agreement. I also emailed a PDF of the letter. In it I stated that during the congressional investigation into the Cobalt ignition switch, the Meltons learned that "GM had fraudulently concealed relevant and critical facts from them, and that at least one GM witness, on whose testimony the Meltons expressly relied in deciding whether to settle their case, had committed perjury in testifying about GM's knowledge of the underlying defects, as well as GM's approval of the design change to the ignition switch in cars other than Brooke's car." I went on to say that we had also learned that GM "had not fully and completely complied with its discovery obligations and had violated Judge Tanksley's February 13, 2013, order to produce documents." As a result, we demanded rescission of the settlement contract because we were going to sue GM for "fraud and deceit, as well as various actions under RICO." RICO is the Racketeer Influenced and Corrupt Organizations Act, which Congress passed in 1970 as a weapon against organized crime. In subsequent years, the justice department used it to combat white-collar crime, and that's what I believed we had here.

In legal terms, this letter was about as subtle as the SWAT team busting through a door. By choosing the words "fraudulently," "perjury," and "RICO," I announced to them that no longer was this a product liability wrongful death case, which was bad enough. Now this case had crossed over into criminal offenses. In their response to our first lawsuit, GM hid behind the distinction between the old, pre-bankruptcy GM and the new, post-bailout GM. They could still claim it was old GM that made the defective ignition switch, although the engineer who designed it still worked for them, but our lawsuit placed the blame for the fraudulent concealment, perjury, and RICO violations squarely on the shoulders of the new GM.

I gave GM until April 20 to respond. On April 19, I received a letter, but not from Phil Holladay or anyone else at King and Spalding. GM's response letter came from Robert Ellis, a partner at the Chicago office of Kirkland and Ellis, which is reputed to be the world's highest-grossing law firm with more than $3 billion a year in revenue. I knew of Kirkland and Ellis. GM normally brought them into cases only when they faced enormous liability exposure.

Ellis's response was short and to the point. GM denied our assertion that they had fraudulently concealed relevant and critical information from us. They also denied engaging in any improper behavior surrounding the settlement agreement. Ellis pointed out that my clients had signed a full and complete release of GM from any and all claims, as well as any future claims against GM. For these reasons, GM not only declined our rescission but also warned they would "vigorously defend any attempt to rescind the settlement in the Melton action, or to relitigate or pursue a new lawsuit related to the Melton matter." As far as GM was concerned, this matter was over and they would fight to keep it that way.

Fortunately for our side, under Georgia law, GM did not have to accept our rescission for it to stand. General Motors' refusal to accept the return of the settlement did not stop us from refiling the lawsuit, which I did on May 12, 2014, along with document requests and interrogatories. In essence, the rescission turns back the clock to where all parties stood before the settlement agreement. By refiling the lawsuit, we picked up where we left off, with some key differences, the first being the way we filed it.

I didn't just go down to the local courthouse and file the lawsuit with the clerk of the court. On the day I filed, I held a press conference attended by all kinds of local and national media. Ken also spoke, and both he and Beth answered questions. Both made it clear they wanted justice not only for Brooke but for all the other families who'd suffered loss because of the dangerous and defective ignition switches.

During the news conference, I made copies of the refiled suit available for the media. The new suit differed substantially from the original. For starters, the original lawsuit was only eleven pages long. The second was fifty-four. I needed that much space to list a thumbnail sketch of what we now knew about GM's actions going back to 2001 when they first discovered problems with the ignition switch. When I filed the original suit, I suspected the power steering system may have had something to do with Brooke's accident, along with an electrical system which allowed the Cobalt to stall and lose power while driving. Three years later, I knew exactly what caused her accident and I spelled it out in great detail.

The range of charges we brought against GM had grown accordingly. The original suit alleged negligence and strict liability, meaning GM was responsible for its defective product. The second added fraudulent concealment. I made the case that GM knew about the safety defects in the Chevrolet Cobalt more than nine years before Brooke's fatal accident, but they "intentionally, purposefully, fraudulently, and systematically" concealed those defects from Brooke, the National Highway Traffic Safety Administration, and the driving public. Harold had dismissed my first suit as nothing more than a fishing expedition. Of course, he was wrong. Neither he nor anyone else could call this second filing a fishing expedition. We had the facts of GM's negligence and concealment. We had indisputable evidence of perjury. We had a judge to whom GM had already lied. Once we received the rest of the documents that chronicled how deeply the corruption within GM ran, we'd have, to say the least, the upper hand. I could not wait to get this case in front of a jury.

Our interrogatories went straight to the heart of the fraud and perjury claims. I asked for the names of each and every person, including lawyers, who met with Ray DeGiorgio either in person or over the phone or by any other means at any time to prepare him for his deposition. I wanted all the documents shown to DeGiorgio, and all documents created by GM and its legal team to assess and deal with DeGiorgio's deposition. And I wanted all of the communications between GM's in-house lawyers and its outside counsel who previously worked on ignition switch claims. I intended to use these documents to prove that GM and its lawyers conspired to cover up the defect all the way back to February 23, 2006, when they settled the first ignition switch claim made by Theresa DiBattista, the mother of Amber Rose, who died on July 29, 2005, when the airbags in her Cobalt did not deploy.

Normally, correspondence between attorneys and clients is privileged and protected from discovery. However, when GM's attorneys at King and Spalding signed off on Ray DeGiorgio's deposition testimony in which he committed perjury, they became a party to his crime. Because of that, all claims of attorney/client privilege became irrelevant. To put it bluntly, fraud is not protected by attorney/client privilege, especially if the legal team was in on the cover-up. That's something we demanded to know.

No sooner had I filed the suit than GM immediately responded with a motion to dismiss. Judge Tanksley scheduled a hearing on their motion for August 9, 2014. I knew GM was going to fight us tooth and nail not just in this hearing but every step along the way. I didn't care. They had stonewalled us and lied to us and done everything in their power to keep the truth hidden. If they wanted a bare-knuckles, no-holds-barred fight, I was more than happy to oblige. Never had the stakes been higher for me. If we lost, I'd have to scrape together my fees that came out of the Meltons' five-million-dollar settlement, money I did not have. But I wasn't thinking in terms of winning and losing. This was about justice, and I was not going to rest until I saw it done.

CHAPTER 16

GM Resets the Narrative

By the time I refiled the Melton case, the ground seemed to be collapsing under General Motors. The ignition switch controversy dominated every news cycle, while the number of lawsuits against them kept growing. Talk of GM's imminent demise spread. If not for a huge bailout by United States taxpayers in 2009, GM would have already gone the way of the Studebaker and DeLorean. People wondered if the company could survive this blow coming only five years later. It wasn't just the potential of billions of dollars of lawsuits that threatened the company's viability. As Mary Barra admitted before Congress, GM had lost the public's trust. Not only did the automaker knowingly place a defective part in millions of cars, they chose to do nothing about it when they first became aware of the problem. Some companies never recover from such a one-two punch.

I never believed GM might actually go out of business. The phrase "too big to fail" had already been thrown about to justify the United States government's bailing out more than just General Motors. During the financial crisis of 2008 and 2009, taxpayers bailed out banks and other businesses for the sake of preserving jobs and keeping the economy stable. There was no way the Obama administration, or any other administration, Democrat or Republican, was going to sit back and let GM go under now, not after already investing billions to keep the company afloat. Members of Congress might posture and make scathing speeches as they already had in the ignition switch House and Senate hearings, but at the end of the day, GM employs more than 200,000 people. No one will ever stand back and let them simply go under. The results across the economy, not just here but around the world, could be devastating.

However, even though I did not think the United States government would allow General Motors to go under, that might be a moot point if the car buying public so lost faith in GM that sales plummeted to the degree that they could not stay in business. No government program can make people buy a certain brand of car, and no amount of catchy jingles and slick advertising campaigns can overcome the perception that you build cars that kill people and you don't care. GM had to reset the narrative and find a way to get out in front of this story before it buried them. And that's exactly what they did.

The Valukas Report

When Mary Barra testified before House and Senate subcommittees, she promised she'd have the results of a "thorough and unimpeded investigation of the actions of General Motors" by Anton Valukas within forty-five to sixty days. "There are no boundaries and there are no sacred cows," she said when it came to the Valukas investigation. "I want to make sure we have a complete understanding, because only with a complete understanding can we make all the changes we need to make from both a people and a process perspective." She called Valukas a man with decades of experience and the highest integrity who would not compromise his reputation for GM.

As I wrote in chapter 14, throughout her testimony, Ms. Barra often claimed ignorance about a matter, explaining that was why Mr. Valukas was conducting his investigation. Needless to say, every member of the committees before which she spoke expressed a desire to get a copy of the Valukas investigation as soon as it was available.

That day came on June 4, 2014, with the release of the 315-page Valukas report. Barra also fired fifteen people the same day as the report's release. Those who lost their jobs included Ray DeGiorgio and Gary Altman. I found it ironic that, given all that had come out since his deposition a year before, Ray DeGiorgio had continued working on switches for GM up until the release of the Valukas report.

At first glance, the Valukas report was all that Mary Barra had promised. News reports the next day called it damning and disturbing. Valukas exposed a "disturbing pattern of incompetence" and a corporate culture with a "proliferation of committees and a lack of accountability." Valukas found that committee after committee met to discuss the ignition switch problem, yet often no notes were taken of the meetings. People told Valukas that problems were flagged, solutions suggested, but that was the end of the matter. They described the "GM salute," which was a crossing of the arms and pointing outward toward others, basically saying that the responsibility to do something belongs to someone else and not me.[5] Mary Barra herself described the "GM nod," which is when everyone nods in agreement that a proposed plan of action needs to be taken, but then everyone leaves the room with no intention of doing anything about it.[6]

The report singles out many people for their failure to act when problems with the ignition switch first surfaced and started to snowball. However, Valukas said he found no evidence of deliberate wrongdoing or a conspiracy to cover up the switch problems, instead blaming the decade-long delay to recall the switch on incompetence and neglect. Valukas chided the company employees for their failure to understand the basic elements of a car the company had designed and manufactured. The company also had a silo organization, where information was not shared between departments, thus prolonging the delay in fixing problems with the switch. Overall, most felt Valukas had laid the company bare, even though he absolved Mary Barra and the executive branch of the company of any wrongdoing. The bureaucracy and bloated corporate structure bore much of the blame, he concluded, but not the people at the top making decisions. There was no fraud, no conspiracy, just a perfect storm of incompetence and lack of accountability that resulted in at least thirteen fatalities.

I didn't buy it. From the day Barra announced she'd hired the man she called a former US attorney, I was skeptical. True, Valukas had been the United States Attorney for the Northern District of Illinois from 1985 to 1989, but since 2007, he'd been the chairman of the Chicago law firm of Jenner and Block. One of Jenner and Block's biggest corporate clients was none other than GM. In November 2011, Jenner and Block served as lead outside counsel to the newly constituted General Motors LLC in its initial public stock offering (IPO). Valukas also brought in King and Spalding to assist him in his "independent" investigation. Mary Barra claimed this investigation would be a no-holds-barred, critical analysis of every part of the company. I wasn't alone in questioning how independent an investigation could be when it was conducted by two firms who had worked for GM for years, and most likely would continue to work for them in the future. Senator Richard Blumenthal of Connecticut called it "the best report money can buy."[7]

My problems with the report went beyond the lack of independence. In terms of the facts about the company, Valukas did not pull any punches. The report was brutal in a lot of ways. However, Valukas accepted at face value the assumption that created the long-term problem with the switch in the first place, and he did so right from the start. In the introductory section, he wrote, "In 2004, however, GM engineers, faced with a multitude of reports of moving stalls caused by the ignition switch, concluded that moving stalls were not safety issues because drivers could still maneuver the cars; they completely failed to understand that the movement of the switch out of the Run position meant the driver and passengers would *no longer have the protection of the airbags.*"[8]

In other words, driving down the highway and hitting a bump, which causes the key to turn the car off, is a safety issue only because it prevents the airbags from deploying in case of an accident. The loss of power steering and antilock brakes and traction control and every other safety system, as well as the very real possibility of the transmission doing a hard downshift, which can cause the front wheels to lock up— everything that happened to Brooke Melton when her key inadvertently turned—none of this in and of itself constitutes a safety issue. The only safety issue is airbags that do not deploy when the key is off.

This same assumption runs throughout Valukas's report. When explaining the mystery of getting to the root of the problem with the Cobalt (which they defined as an airbag nondeployment problem), Valukas writes, "Investigators, convinced that the cause of the airbag nondeployments was a complicated mystery still to be unraveled, failed to consider fully the simple, and ultimately correct, cause: the switch that caused cars to stall was turning the power off and disabling the airbags just as cars were about to crash."[9] The question he never addresses, much less answers, is the one that should have driven the investigation: Why did these drivers lose control of their cars and crash in the first place? Whether anyone ever stopped and asked if there might be a connection between engine stalls and the accidents where the airbags did not deploy is something Valukas evidently did not feel needed to be explored.

At the end of his report, Valukas chides GM as he writes, "The failures from 2011 to 2013 demonstrate a lack of urgency in the face of a pattern of airbag failures, an unwillingness by GM personnel to re-evaluate their conclusions, a lack of accountability or leadership in driving the investigations to a conclusion, and a continued reluctance to elevate issues."[10] I agree with the conclusion regarding the lack of urgency, accountability, and leadership. However, by ignoring the inherent danger in a moving stall that disables critical safety features in a vehicle, Valukas himself fails to elevate what should be the primary issue with the switch. Moving stalls made these vehicles unsafe to drive and contributed to accidents, many of them fatal. That the airbags failed to deploy only compounded a potentially fatal situation.

The unwillingness by anyone associated in any way with GM, including the man who investigated the Cobalt switch fiasco, to question the idea that a moving stall in and of itself is a safety issue is, I believe, one of the primary reasons our case proved to be so problematic for them. The Valukas report misrepresented the facts of our case. When Valukas turned to "The Melton Evaluation," he described the facts of the case in this way:

> The Melton case arose out of a two-car crash that occurred on March 10, 2010, in Georgia. Brooke Melton was driving her 2005 Cobalt through heavy rain when she encountered standing water in the roadway. Melton, who the accident report said was driving too fast for the conditions, lost control of her car, veered sideways into the southbound travel lane, and was struck on the passenger side by another vehicle. Melton's Cobalt then traveled rear first off the roadway and dropped approximately fifteen feet into a creek with rising water from the rain. According to the SDM data, at the time of the accident, the vehicle's power mode status was in Accessory.[11]

Their argument was based on a central fallacy. Brooke did not drive into standing water. Eyewitnesses testified that the so-called "heavy rain" was more of a mist, or at most a sprinkle. Nor was there standing water left over from earlier rains. We checked into that at the very beginning and found that water did not pool on the road in question. While the police report did say she was driving too fast for conditions, our experts concluded she lost control of her car because it dropped from run to accessory.

There was more. The report quoted the Melton matter roundtable where GM legal staff attorney Ronald Porter addressed the issue of how the power mode in Brooke's Cobalt ended up in accessory:

> At this time we have identified 3 possible explanations for the accessory position data. 1. Melton turned the key to the accessory

position. This might have occurred if she was attempting to restart the engine after it stalled. 2. Ignition circuit "bounce." FPA has seen a few instances involving Cobalts operated on rough roads where the ignition circuit goes to the accessory position due to vibration. 3. *Interference from the poorly designed and poorly installed after-market alarm system.* This might have been the cause of the stalling condition for which Melton took the car to [the dealer] several days before the crash.[12]

Two years after we demonstrated that the DEI alarm system had nothing to do with Brooke's accident, it was back in the forefront. While the Valukas report did not directly blame the security system, including this quote inferred that something beyond the switch may have played a role. This quote also demonstrated GM still could not bring itself to acknowledge that the defective ignition switch caused Brooke Melton's death. To paraphrase Pete Townsend from the legendary rock band The Who, "Meet the new GM, same as the old GM."

GM's disdain for us carried over into Anton Valukas's appearance before Congress shortly after the report's release. Representative Phil Gingrey of Georgia, who represented Brooke's congressional district, asked Valukas directly, "If not for the Brooke Melton lawsuit . . . and the fact that her lawyers figured out that the ignition switch part from model year 2008 was different from model years 2005, [200]6 and [200]7 in the Cobalt, would we even know about this ignition switch problem today? Would we even be aware of it?"

Valukas replied, "The answer is yes because the—there was an open and at that point significant investigation going on at that—at that particular point. And certainly, there was information and evidence that was accumulating as they were going forward pointing to the fact that they had these nondeployments, pointing to the fact that they had fatalities and pointing to the fact that the switch had something to do with it."

To which Representative Gingrey promptly replied, "Well, that smacks of a big cover-up to me." It smacked of that and more to me. Listening to Valukas once again downplay the role of the Melton lawsuit in bringing GM's dirty little secret to light, and in doing so, once again imply that *Melton* didn't even apply because the only real issue was airbag nondeployment, just made me angry.

My other immediate issue with the Valukas report can be summed up by this headline that appeared in *Fortune* a few days after the report's release: "How one rogue employee can upend a whole company."[13] The running narrative of the report reads like a detective novel, a real whodunit. And the answer Valukas finds is that the one most responsible for keeping the problem with the ignition switch from coming to light sooner was the man who designed it, Ray DeGiorgio.

As early as Groundhog Day 2002, DeGiorgio knew that the detent force in the switch did not meet the minimum requirement of 20 N-cm. In an email to Erik Mattson of Delphi Corporation (which built the production model of the switch), DeGiorgio tells Mattson, "If increasing the detent ACCRY force by 5N will destroy this switch than (sic) do nothing . . . maintain present course. Under no circumstances do we want to compromise the electrical performance of this switch." He then signs the email, "Ray (tired of the switch from hell) DeGiorgio."[14]

As the narrative of the switch continues through the report, DeGiorgio consistently stands out as the one who blocks any design changes. He hid the fact that the switch was substandard, even though others had to sign off on the tests run on the switch. When the time came to put the switch into production or redesign it to meet specifications, according to the Valukas report, DeGiorgio alone instructed Delphi to use his design without changes. Later, when problems inevitably arose and the question was asked if the detent force could be increased, DeGiorgio claimed such changes would take up to two years to implement and cost hundreds of thousands of dollars. When the switch was secretly changed, the Valukas report makes it sound like DeGiorgio acted alone. He made the design change, and he alone sent the change in plans to Delphi, instructing them not to change the part number of the new switch. Yes, a culture of buck passing, lack of accountability, and general incompetence contributed to GM's downfall, but Valukas placed the weight of the blame upon Ray DeGiorgio. One bad apple truly did spoil the entire bunch as DeGiorgio became the fall guy.

The problem with the story that a rogue engineer hijacked the entire company and single-handedly created and concealed a problem costing them billions of dollars is that it ignores the reality of the way in which General Motors, or any other large corporation, actually operates. DeGiorgio did not have final say when it came to approving a defective part for use in millions of cars. Nor did he have final say in not changing the switch and then secretly changing it but leaving the part number the same. He had layers of supervisors over him who had to sign off on all his decisions. Could they have simply waved the switch through with the GM salute and nod? Possibly. But that does not absolve those who did so of responsibility. DeGiorgio was not responsible for a full decade of committees studying the switch without ever taking action to fix it. That blame falls upon the senior management, yet Valukas absolved them of blame. The rogue employee bringing down a 200,000-employee corporation made for interesting reading, but it was far too convenient to be true.

And yet the Valukas report did exactly what it was designed to do. GM presented this scathing self-examination for all the world to see. Mary Barra went back before Congress shortly after its release and answered difficult questions. The report included recommendations for changes that would keep this sort of problem from happening again, and Barra was adamant she and all the leaders of GM were committed to following them. Leadership was dedicated to a culture change within the company. Rather than hide behind the GM nod, she told Congress she now encouraged people to speak up about potential safety issues with an incentive program rewarding whistleblowers. She fell on her sword and the narrative began to change. Now, rather than hiding problems, GM had aired its dirty laundry for all the world to see. We are a changed company, she essentially said, and to prove it, she had taken another step designed to change the public's perception of General Motors and their response to this problem from which they'd run for more than a decade.

The Feinberg Plan

In addition to Mary Barra's announcing during her April appearances before Congress that she'd hired Anton Valukas to investigate the company, she also announced that Kenneth Feinberg had been hired as a consultant. Feinberg was to evaluate the switch situation and recommend the best path forward. Previously he had overseen the victim compensation funds after 9/11, the Boston Marathon bombing, and the Deepwater Horizon oil spill in the Gulf of Mexico. Although she didn't say it at the time, Barra inferred some sort of victims' compensation plan may be on the way for GM.

On June 30, just three and a half weeks after the release of the Valukas report, Feinberg announced that a compensation fund had been set up for victims of accidents caused by the defective ignition switch. The fund featured different levels of payment based on the severity of the injuries and the victim's age, earning potential, medical expenses, and family obligations. Payments to the families of those who had died would start at $1 million and go up from there. Feinberg, not GM, would have the final say about who was paid what. The fund also did not have a cap, nor would the 2009 bankruptcy agreements impact who could make a claim. As if to emphasize how serious GM was about making things right, Feinberg said that the claims process would not factor in things like speeding, driving while intoxicated, whether the injured parties were wearing their seat belts, or whether they were texting or distracted in some other way. If the switch caused the accident or the airbags failed to deploy, victims would be compensated. Applications for compensation were scheduled to begin on August 1, 2014, and run through early 2015. All those accepting payment from the fund had to sign a legal document waiving their right to sue in the future.

From the start, the Feinberg fund, even more than the Valukas report, changed the public perception of GM and the ignition switch controversy. Rather than the villain who callously sat by while people died as a result of a defective product, GM was now front and center, not only admitting fault but doing their best to make things right with those they had harmed. By having Feinberg, rather than a mediator from GM, set the size of the compensation award, this process had the appearance of independence. In the news conference where Feinberg gave the details of the plan, he mentioned that while GM had approved his plan, it wasn't happy that the compensation fund was not capped. Essentially, GM had signed a blank check that Feinberg could fill out as he saw fit.

The Feinberg fund ended up being a brilliant decision by GM. GM faced potentially thousands of lawsuits alleging that the defective ignition switches in GM cars caused fatalities and catastrophic injuries. The last thing GM wanted to do was to see those families in court where a jury would decide GM's fate. Feinberg encouraged victims to submit a claim and even told them if they didn't like the compensation he thought was appropriate, they could turn him down and take GM to court. Almost all of those eligible submitted claims to Feinberg and chose to accept his settlement offer. Of course, each had their own reasons for settling their claims. But from what I could tell, the overarching reason was that they did not want to deal with what they and their attorneys knew would be a long-drawn-out fight with GM.

One thing we knew for certain: despite GM's public statements that they now accepted responsibility for the ignition switch debacle, they intended to fight every lawsuit with whatever means they had at their disposal.

CHAPTER 17

My Super Bowl

I don't know if I've ever been more ready to step into a courtroom and dreading it at the same time.

Everything rode on the outcome of this hearing. GM had filed a motion to dismiss the second Melton lawsuit. If Judge Tanksley ruled in their favor, that was it. Game over. There'd be no trial, no chance publicly to press our charges of fraud. While the settlement to which we agreed nearly a year earlier was probably not in jeopardy, we wanted the whole truth to come out, not GM's spin on the truth. The stakes could not be higher.

Unlike the hearings before the judge during the first Melton suit, I was not alone against GM's team of lawyers. The Beasley Allen law firm partnered with me when I refiled the suit, and they were with me on this day, including the founding partner, Jere Beasley. Jere, the former lieutenant governor of Alabama, started the firm as a one-man operation in 1979. Since then he'd become one of the most respected attorneys in the country. In 2004 he won an $11.8 billion suit against ExxonMobil on behalf of the state of Alabama. Greg Allen, Ben Baker, Ken Bernard, and two others rounded out our legal team.

Brian Sieve of Kirkland and Ellis out of Chicago led GM's team, which included a lawyer named Robert Ingram and two other local Cobb County attorneys. Robert is a good friend, but I knew Sieve was running the show for GM's legal team now. By dumping Phil Holladay and Harold Franklin of King and Spalding in favor of Sieve, GM signaled it would spare no expense in its efforts to stop us in our tracks.

Cameras and microphones from news crews both local and national lined the steps of the courthouse when we arrived. Inside the courtroom wasn't much better. Judge Tanksley had allowed the media to be present for the hearing, which only heightened the tension. As my team made its way into the courtroom, we didn't make any kind of small talk with the other side. Sieve looked over at us with a dismissive look. I'm sure he was thinking we shouldn't even be having this hearing. I felt confident that our refiling of the lawsuit stood on solid legal ground, but you never know what may happen when you step inside a courtroom. Butterflies fluttered in my stomach.

"You okay?" Jere asked as we sat down.

"Yeah," I said. "Just ready to get this out of the way and get on with preparing for trial."

"Don't worry," Jere reassured me. "They don't have a leg to stand on."

I hoped Jere was right. Any nervousness I felt evaporated pretty quickly when Judge Tanksley opened up the proceedings by saying, "The first order of business is we're serving you today with a notice that this trial—that this case has been set for April 11, 2016, beginning at nine o'clock, for trial. It will continue day-to-day until a verdict is reached. Also, I've set down a pretrial hearing for that trial on March 21st, 2016, at 10:30 a.m. And based on those dates, the counsel for all parties are instructed to submit a Proposed Consent Scheduling Order by September 30th, with specific deadlines for enumerated items in the order, and others that may be needed not limited to those. Thank you.

"I'm ready to hear your motions, and I would like to know who's going to speak on behalf of the defendant, General Motors."

I glanced toward my partners, trying hard not to grin. I could hardly believe what had just happened. Neither side had presented any oral arguments, only briefs presenting our sides, and yet she'd just told us when the trial was going to start, along with all the other pertinent dates connected to it. This was huge. In not so subtle terms, she had already telegraphed her decision to us, and it was not going to be good for GM. The motion to dismiss would be denied and GM would be staring at a jury on April 11, 2016. I'm sure Sieve picked up on this too, although his demeanor did not change.

Robert Ingram kicked things off by pleading GM's case for dismissing the suit. Ingram's argument was simple: The new suit brought the same causes of action as the original suit, but that case had already been settled. Therefore, we could not file a new suit based on *res judicata*, which is a Latin term that means "a matter already judged." In legalese, *res judicata* means that a case that has already been judged and settled cannot be brought up again without first setting aside the decision of the first court. When we settled the first Melton case, we executed a settlement agreement with GM. Judge Tanksley's court then dismissed that case with prejudice. For us to refile, both settlement agreements had to be set aside and Judge Tanksley had to dismiss her dismissal. Essentially, since we had not done that, this new suit must therefore be thrown out. Ingram cited case law and legal precedents where *res judicata* trumped rescission. Therefore, he argued, the court had no choice but to dismiss this case.

I then stood and made my case. Basically, I argued that the previous agreement we had entered into was based on fraud. At least one GM witness, namely Ray DeGiorgio, had perjured himself in his deposition. GM's legal representation from King and Spalding suborned this fraudulent testimony, as did GM, by telling us no records existed of anyone in the company approving a change to the ignition switch. I didn't just make this argument. I showed video of DeGiorgio's testimony. I then argued that before we went to trial in the first suit, we should have known GM changed the switch years before Brooke's accident, and that they could have changed it in Brooke's car. We therefore settled under false pretenses, which was our reason for the rescission.

As for the matter of *res judicata*, I cited Georgia statutes and case law to show that rescission takes precedent over *res judicata*. Since we were fraudulently induced into settling, we did not have to first go and do anything else before we pleaded rescission. The settlement agreement was a private matter between the Meltons and GM that was not ordered by a judge. We did have to agree to a dismissal afterward for GM, but only because the lawsuit against Thornton continued. That was a procedural hoop we had to jump through for that part of the suit to continue. The dismissal didn't change the fact that the private agreement with GM had been based on a lie on their part. This motion to dismiss should therefore be denied.

Then it was Brian Sieve's turn to speak. Like Ingram, he argued *res judicata*, claiming this case had been judged and settled. Until and unless the earlier judgment was set aside, this new suit could not continue, he argued. His arguments all rested on procedural grounds. He never denied allegations of fraud. Instead he acted as if the allegations were irrelevant. He argued we hadn't jumped through the right hoops in the right order. Until we did, we could not refile this lawsuit.

Judge Tanksley was having none of it. She started asking questions, the tone of which made it clear that she disagreed with their arguments. At one point she asked, "Well, let's just do it this way. You tell me how we would have gone about doing this?" Later during her questions and answers with Sieve, before she'd ruled on the motion, she said to him she couldn't see how *res judicata* would keep this case from going forward.

I knew right then that we had carried the day, but Sieve was not ready to concede. He claimed that the settlement into which we entered covered the new allegations of fraud. "The original claims a product liability case with respect to the underlying vehicle, and so the fraudulent concealment count, as I read it in count four [of the new Melton suit], was simply that you failed to disclose a defect, which Mr. Cooper claims General Motors was aware of and should have disclosed earlier. So to me, as I read that, those are all part of the same count. Those are claims that could have been brought in *Melton I*, that's what *res judicata* is," Sieve argued.

Judge Tanksley fired right back, "How could he have known? Mary Barra didn't know. How's he going to know?"

"Well, he alleges that—" Sieve started to reply.

Judge Tanksley cut him off. "The CEO of GM testified in front of Congress that she didn't know. Are you going to hold the Meltons to a higher standard than GM?"

Sieve tried again to assert that any new claims of fraudulent concealment we now alleged should have been brought in the first case, and were thus invalid now, but Judge Tanksley was having none of it. "The only way he could have brought those claims in the first lawsuit," she said, "is to have known something that the executives at GM claim they didn't know. I mean, that's simple. I can't see it any other way."

Not surprisingly, a short time later, Judge Tanksley ruled in our favor. This case was back on. We had a year and a half until our trial date, but I knew it would take that long to go through the documents I expected to receive soon. Judge Tanksley gave GM fifteen days to produce everything we had asked for in our interrogatories and requests for documents. Given the way GM had held back before, I knew she would not tolerate anything short of complete compliance. This felt like a huge victory.

Sadly, the thrill would be short lived.

CHAPTER 18

The Handwriting
on the Wall

I didn't have time to savor Judge Tanksley's favorable ruling. I had to fly out to New York the next day, a Sunday, for an important hearing Monday morning before Judge Jesse Furman in the Second District of New York federal court. Some of the nearly one hundred GM cases on which I'd partnered with Beasley Allen had been rolled into what is known as multidistrict litigation (MDL), along with thousands of ignition switch related lawsuits from across the country. An MDL is formed by a panel of judges whenever multiple civil actions share one or more common issues against one entity. The panel assigned the MDL to Judge Furman in New York because the GMC bankruptcy had taken place in New York back in 2009.

I didn't have a lot of experience with MDLs, but a team from Beasley Allen brought me up to speed. An MDL is unique. In some ways, it is like a class action lawsuit because a single court exercises oversight of the discovery process for all the cases brought together under its umbrella under the leadership of co-lead attorneys and an executive committee appointed by Judge Furman. However, unlike a class action suit, the individual cases remain distinct entities. Practically speaking, this means GM produces one set of documents for Judge Furman's court, and those documents then become available for all the cases in the MDL. Witnesses are deposed only once with the video of their testimonies available to every case. If and when an individual case goes to trial, it returns to where it was originally filed and is tried there by the attorneys who filed it.

All of this is supposed to create an "All for one and one for all" synergy for the attorneys with cases in the MDL. In the real world, that's not exactly how it works. To borrow a sentiment from Orwell's *Animal Farm*, all the attorneys in an MDL are equal, but some are more equal than others. The most equal in terms of overall power were the co-lead attorneys, with the executive committee right below them. Not only did the co-leads control the discovery process, they, in conjunction with Judge Furman and GM's legal team, also determined the order in which the individual cases were heard. But that's only the tip of their power.

The MDL orders usually grant the co-leads a percentage of any settlement reached in every case of the MDL, with a lesser amount going to the executive committee. In this case, with thousands of suits all rolled together, GM faced paying out potentially *billions* in settlements, which meant the co-leads stood to receive tens of millions of dollars to split between them simply because of their position over the MDL. Needless to say, these economic incentives made a co-lead position highly coveted.

Survivor

The night before the hearing where Judge Furman was to select the MDL leadership team, I attended a dinner with around twenty-five to thirty attorneys, all of whom were vying for one of the top spots. While I am not naïve enough to think we were all going to join hands and sing "Kum Ba Yah," I wasn't prepared for the level of cutthroat, dog-eat-dog one-upmanship playing out around the room. Instead of gathering around a campfire, I felt like I'd just walked into a scene from the movie *The Godfather.*

I walked around the room to try to get my bearings. All around me, lawyers huddled talking strategy and discussing alliances, like a game of legal *Survivor* with a ballroom rather than an island as the setting. Many approached me because I was already in a position of power. The temporary co-leads recommended Judge Furman appoint me to the executive committee, which made that pretty much a slam dunk. A few talked to me privately before the dinner and told me I should push to be one of the co-leads. "Look, you uncovered all of this. Not one of us would be here if it weren't for you and what you uncovered with *Melton*. If you ask, the judge is going to make you a co-lead. No doubt about it." I was told this more than once. Each time my response was the same: I felt I didn't know enough about the MDL process to be a lead. Looking back, I should have listened.

As the night wore on and I talked to more people, I discovered that everyone in the room had withdrawn their applications to be a co-lead. Instead, they all sought another leadership position. I found that very curious until someone explained what was going on. Furman had appointed three people as temporary co-leads: Mark Robinson, Steve Berman, and Elizabeth Cabraser. He picked them because they had been the co-leads in a huge MDL involving Toyota that had recently settled. That's how these things work. The same people get recycled through leadership positions over and over again. If you stood up and applied to be a co-lead, you basically said Furman made a mistake and would therefore alienate the co-leads if Furman turned you down. I quickly learned these MDL lawyers did not want to alienate others because there were sure to be future cases to work on and lots of money to be made.

So now, instead of challenging for a co-lead position, most people in the room were campaigning for a position on the executive committee. By the time the night ended, we all left knowing that Robinson, Berman, and Cabraser were going to remain co-leads and that I was going to be on the executive committee. Everything else was up in the air.

The next morning, when I arrived at Judge Furman's court, I noticed one guy who had been absent the night before. When I asked about him, I discovered he was Robert Hilliard out of the Houston, Texas, area. I recognized the name. Right after I refiled *Melton*, he'd called me telling me he represented the family of Amy Rademaker. He went on to ask if I'd consider partnering with him on these and future cases against GM. "Together we'll go in there and kick GM's ass and take no prisoners," he said. Personally, I was put off by his bombastic approach. We talked two or three times by phone, but in the end, I decided to pass. From what I could tell, I didn't think we'd make a good team.

I never saw him in person, nor did I speak to him again until I spotted him in Judge Furman's courtroom. Unlike every other attorney in the room, he appeared to be all alone. He hadn't been a part of the deal-cutting, alliance-forming bull session the night before. When I asked someone next to me about him, they dismissed him by saying, "Yeah, I saw where he is applying for a co-lead. He'll never get it. He's not connected to anyone with influence in this thing. Don't worry about him. He's not getting anything." Me, I wasn't so sure.

Judge Furman called the morning session to order by laying out how the MDL process would play out in his court. He briefly discussed the hundreds of cases from state and federal courts that were included in this MDL, but that soon moved to a discussion of the significant cases which were not a part of it. *Melton* was at the top of the list. I fought and won to keep *Melton* separate. It didn't fit here. All these other cases focused on the ignition switch and GM's hiding the problems with it for a decade. Only the Melton case added allegations of fraud against the "new" GM in how they initially settled with my clients.

Part of the discussion during the morning session turned to interrogatories and document requests. My ears perked up when my Melton case came up. The judge asked Mark Robinson, "What bearing does that have on our proceedings here, or in your view can it proceed on a separate track, Mr. Robinson?"

Since Mark Robinson represented the plaintiffs, I expected him to say something like, "The Melton case is not in the MDL, so it should proceed on a separate track." His answer was, "I think that actually it is a state court case . . . [and since] there is discovery going on in that case [i.e., discovery of new information, it] may be something the court may want to consider. I would like to reserve that [decision] until we get to discovery."

He wanted to wait to answer until the MDL moved into discovery. Why? I wondered. The hairs on the back of my neck stood up. I tried to tell myself this was nothing to worry about, but something told me I shouldn't be so sure.

Then Rick Godfrey, who represented GM at the hearing, added his two cents' worth. Not surprisingly, he questioned Judge Tanksley's decision to deny their motion to dismiss two days earlier. Then he added, "The lawyers for the Meltons are in the jurisdiction of this court. The Beasley Allen firm has eight cases here in total. Mr. Cooper has five cases here in total. They are subject to this MDL. Mr. Cooper is seeking a position and has been recommended by temporary lead counsel to have a position on the executive committee. In terms of coordination, the court, as Judge Gerber put it on May 2, may not control other courts but certainly control parties and their counsel." That is, while the Melton case was not under the jurisdiction of the court, I and my partners from Beasley Allen were. I did not see how that mattered. Godfrey did.

"It is a difference in viewpoint to suggest the Melton case does not involve new GM conduct," Godfrey continued. "The Melton case is designed to set aside the settlement so they can sue over the allegations involving Mr. DeGiorgio and what old GM did, et cetera, and very much involves the same discovery, the same issues here." Basically, this means he thought *Melton* should be a part of the MDL. "That is all I have to say about *Melton*," he concluded, "but I do think there is an inherent challenge of coordination between this MDL and the lawyers appearing in this MDL for other parties in those and those same lawyers, the discovery that they seek in a case which we find indistinguishable in the state court of Cobb County, Georgia."

Listening to Robinson and then Godfrey, I could not help but wonder what I had gotten myself into. I started to think I'd made a mistake being here and having any cases in this MDL. I tried to convince myself I was worrying about nothing, and I succeeded. By the time the afternoon session rolled around, I felt better about everything. Even with all the positioning the night before, at the end of the day we were all on the same team. We didn't even know who was going to be the co-leads or on the executive committee. I was getting ahead of myself jumping to conclusions now.

Looking back, I realize my instincts were right. Of course, by the time I understood what was happening, it was too late.

Legal Beauty Pageant

The morning session dragged on until 1:15 p.m. Promptly at 2:00, Judge Furman reconvened his court to consider all those who had applied for a leadership position. Forty people had requested an opportunity to make their case before the judge, and all forty were given their chance. To keep from showing any hint of favoritism, Judge Furman lined us up alphabetically, giving each one of us exactly four minutes. He even pulled out his phone, set a four-minute timer complete with alarm, and told us before the first person got up to speak that when we heard the alarm we were to step down. To keep things moving along quickly, when he called someone up to speak, he alerted whoever was next in line to get in the on-deck circle and be ready to start as soon as the other person ended.

Then, beginning with Alexander and with Bailey on deck, the legal beauty pageant began in earnest. I don't know what else to call what ensued over the next two and a half hours. One after another, attorneys of all shapes and sizes and races, male and female, stood up and sang their own praises. They talked about the huge verdicts they'd won and the honors they'd received. Judge Furman instructed everyone to state how many cases he or she had in this particular MDL, and I quickly realized this was an important factor. I found the whole thing distasteful.

However I felt about the process, if I wanted to be a part of the leadership team, I had to get up and sing my own praises as well. Since I had no experience in an MDL, my argument for being appointed to the executive committee came down to my experience and expertise gained in the Melton case. I said, "My commitment to this case is this: No law firm has been more committed to this litigation over the last four years than our law firm . . . Simply put, our firm knows more about the key system defects in this case than any firm in the country . . . Given our previous work, we have a team of experts in place. We have already spent hundreds of thousands of dollars on experts to assist co-lead counsel in prosecuting this case. If appointed to an executive committee position, our firm would be in a position to coordinate with other counsel, to efficiently and effectively represent the interests of all clients, both economic class and personal injury and wrongful death clients."

I then closed by being very open about my lack of experience with MDLs. "I have never applied for an MDL position before," I said. "Our firm has no prior experience as lead counsel, court appointed in MDL cases. We have handled cases in MDL," I said before going to the heart of my argument, "but we have lived this case the last four years, and since we respectfully submit we uncovered these key system defects, we would like an opportunity to be part of a leadership team that finishes what our firm started. Thank you."

To my surprise, the attorneys from GM commented on my presentation. "We believe Mr. Cooper should be a part of the executive committee," they said. I immediately wondered why they would do that. I felt a little like George Bailey when Mr. Potter offers to hire him away from the Bailey Building and Loan. There had to be more to their agreeing to have me be on the executive committee than met the eye.

As the day wore on and more attorneys spoke, everyone stuck to the plan from the night before. No one other than the acting temporary co-leads requested a co-lead attorney position; that is, until Bob Hilliard got up to speak. Hilliard opened with, "Per your court's order, we have filed directly into this MDL 622 cases." I knew Hilliard had filed a number of cases, but I had no idea it was 622. I knew all 622 could not be viable. I knew this from all the potential cases the team from Beasley Allen and I rejected. On average, I'd say we accepted only one out of every five people who contacted us. Hilliard did the opposite. He hired an advertising firm which inundated media markets around the country. As a result, he and his partners signed up hundreds of cases without vetting a one. Now I understood why. He was banking on the sheer number of cases he represented to sway Judge Furman to make him a co-lead. This beauty pageant had taken an ugly turn.

Hilliard also focused on the fact that he was a personal injury attorney. Many of the attorneys in the MDL assumed these cases should focus upon the economic impact of the ignition switch problems, meaning the resale value that every car owner lost because of the recall. The argument was, with all of the bad news about GM and the fact that they had recalled tens of millions of cars, these cars were now worth less than they should have been and that's what we should go after. Berman and the others believed we should focus on recovering the money these car owners hypothetically lost.

I didn't see it that way. How does anyone quantify how much they actually lost from a possible lower resale value? Also, GM had recalled the cars, but they recalled them to repair them. Once the repairs were made, the resale value should be the same as it would have been if a recall had not been needed. I could not understand how such fuzzy math could claim to be the same sort of damage as someone who had been injured or killed.

Hilliard saw things the same way I did, and he spoke up about it. In pleading his case to become a co-lead, he focused on his position as a personal injury lawyer. That's the kind of leadership he brought to the table, he argued. Others could focus on the economic issues, but he was the man to lead the personal injury parts of the litigation.

When the beauty pageant finally came to an end, I remember telling one of the guys from Beasley Allen who was also at the meeting that I thought Furman was going to pick Hilliard as a co-lead. "There's no way, Lance. Furman is going to stick with the co-leads he originally appointed," I was told.

But I was right. When Judge Furman announced his choices for the permanent co-lead attorneys, he replaced Mark Robinson with Bob Hilliard. What Hilliard did was force Judge Furman's hand. Since Hilliard had by far the most cases in the MDL, Furman basically had to make him a co-lead.

At the time, the decision didn't matter to me one way or another. I had a trial for which I needed to prepare. GM was supposed to begin producing documents for me right away. When I returned home and began requesting specific documents, I received a surprising answer. Brian Sieve's office told me in no uncertain terms that I could not request these documents directly. All of my discovery process first had to go through Judge Furman's court per my position on the MDL executive committee.

GM had found a way to hamstring me, after all.

CHAPTER 19

Nothing Left to Prove

"This court does not have an MDL federal-state coordination problem. It has an MDL lawyer problem," Richard Godfrey, of Kirkland and Ellis, and GM's lead attorney in Judge Furman's court, said during the September 5, 2014, hearing. Given all the pushback I'd received from him regarding production of documents and scheduling depositions over the past few weeks, I was waiting for him to say something like this, but it still grabbed my attention. *Well, let's see if he goes where I think he's going*, I thought.

"What we have here are the cases where discovery is being pressed by an executive member of the MDL's steering committee and by another law firm. Two lawyers in a law firm and another lawyer in this case are pressing all of the state discovery issues. Your Honor ruled last time no deposition discovery. We have gotten a letter from Mr. Cooper, who says *Melton* is independent. He is not controlled by the MDL. He wants depositions at the end of October, beginning of November," Godfrey continued.

Yep, I thought. He might as well have shouted the words "an executive member of the MDL's steering committee," because they went right to the heart of the trap he'd set back in the August 11 hearing and decided to spring now. Even though the refiled Melton case was not part of the MDL, Godfrey wanted Judge Furman to control it because I was a part of the MDL leadership team.

"It will not work if MDL lawyers, subject to the jurisdiction of this court, when the court rules and sets a schedule that we all have to live with, feel unconstrained and unbounded because they can go off to their own state court. That will not work. This is not a state court problem. This is not Judge Tanksley in Cobb County, Georgia, who is setting the schedule. It is Mr. Cooper and the Beasley Allen firm," Godfrey said with the payoff pitch.

Less than a month after he and the rest of the GM legal team said they thought it a good idea for me to be on the executive committee, their motivation for that move was out in the open. They knew they could not control Judge Tanksley and force her to tie my hands. Instead, they bypassed her, arguing now that Judge Furman needed to get this problem, namely me, under control.

"The question, quite frankly, as we said in our letter, is who is going to control the vast, vast majority of the cases, the federal MDL or the State Court of Cobb County? It is not even the state court. That is unfair to Judge Tanksley. It really is. It is the lawyers for a family that previously got a substantial payment and is now settling damages because they are claiming discovery fraud. I understand their claim. GM does not agree with the claim. It is a fundamental problem for this court, as illustrated by the request for deposition," Godfrey said.

Who is going to control the vast, vast majority of cases? Wow. The line sounded like something out of a comic book movie. Godfrey now painted me as the villain about to rip all authority out of Judge Furman's hands not just over the Melton case but over the entire MDL. He'd basically said, "Who is going to run this thing, Judge, you or some hick lawyer from Cobb County, Georgia?"

Godfrey kept talking, making his case that the federal MDL should take priority over every state court case, even those not a part of this MDL, especially *Melton*. But it wasn't the cases that needed to come under the control of Judge Furman's court; it was me. According to him, I presented a problem not just to GM but to the integrity of the notion of multidistrict litigation as laid down by an act of Congress. Over and over Godfrey expressed shock that I could even assert the independence of a case that was not part of the MDL. "I have never been in an MDL where the state courts dictate the schedule for the federal, particularly where it is the same lawyers," he said in a variation of something he'd said multiple times. What I as a part of the MDL leadership team was doing was not only unprecedented according to Godfrey but dangerous. Clearly, I had to be stopped.

The danger I presented to General Motors had nothing to do with asserting the independence of *Melton*, but everything to do with the nature of the refiled case. Our entire case against GM came down to one thing: fraud. GM and their legal teams had misled not only me and Ken and Beth but also Judge Tanksley. From the start they lied to us until forced to tell the truth. First they told us they'd never had problems with a switch that they knew was bad years before they placed it in the first Cobalt. Then they misled us about the changes to the switch, even after confronted with visual evidence of the differences between the old switch and the new. Ray DeGiorgio sat at the deposition, under oath, and said he had no idea how the detent plunger could have grown a tenth of an inch, nor if that change would have any effect on the switch torque levels.

But it wasn't just DeGiorgio who lied about the switch. On up the chain of command, every witness from GM that we confronted with the switch change denied any change had ever been authorized, much less documented. They lied about other switch related accidents and fatalities. The entire three-year process of the Melton lawsuit consisted of us pushing through their lies, obstructions, stonewalling, and perjury.

Because I alleged fraud, I went after a different set of documents than what had been produced in the first go-round, and distinct from what the leadership team of the MDL needed. I requested all the documents GM had claimed were privileged; that is, the communication between GM leadership and both their internal and external legal counsel. Under normal circumstances, those documents were indeed privileged. However, we charged that the attorneys representing GM were in on the fraud, which is why their internal communications with one another and with GM leadership were subject to the discovery process in *Melton*. Attorney-client privilege ends when a crime has been committed by the two of them together. It wasn't just the documents I went after. I planned on deposing the leadership of GM, all the way up to the CEO herself, Mary Barra.

Producing privileged documents and allowing us to depose these high-level GM witnesses were the last things GM intended to let happen. Judge Tanksley had already ordered them to turn the documents over to us by the end of September, and no one from GM's legal team was going to change her mind. That's why GM's lawyers wanted me on the MDL executive committee. It was all about maintaining control, something they never had during the first Melton lawsuit.

And to my surprise, GM's lawyers weren't the only ones who wanted to control me.

MDL Battle

Because I'd never been a part of the leadership team of an MDL before, I did not know exactly how the process might play out. However, I have worked with attorneys from other firms numerous times over the years as we went up against a common foe. While the occasional turf battle might break out, at the end of the day, we were on the same side. Helping our clients is what mattered most. As the old saying goes, a rising tide lifts all boats.

I expected more of the same with the MDL. Because I knew more than anyone else about GM ignition switch problems and how GM covered them up, I had a lot to offer the rest of the team. More than that, I expected to uncover even more in the discovery process of the refiled Melton suit that could make the rest of the MDL cases even stronger. At the very least, proving that GM committed fraud during the first Melton lawsuit made it less likely they would attempt to conceal and deceive this time around. We had GM on the ropes, and I planned to up the pressure to keep it that way.

However, when I pressed for discovery documents and GM balked, the MDL co-leads seemed to side with GM. "You need to funnel every request through us first," all three told me more times than I cared to count. "Whatever documents are produced need to go through Judge Furman."

"Why?" I kept asking. "I have a judge who knows far more about this litigation than Judge Furman, and she's also shown she's not going to put up with any games or delays. If I can get the evidence now through her, that's going to help us in the MDL cases. But if I have to wait for all these document requests to work their way through the federal MDL red tape, the delay will hurt my prep for my Melton trial."

In not so many words, I was told none of that mattered. When I kept pushing back, one of the co-leads, Steve Berman out of Washington, basically told me, "You don't get it, Lance. Our case, the federal case, is going to run the show from now on." I found it odd that Berman was even a co-lead since he rarely took a case all the way to trial and usually settled out of court instead. How then could he possibly know the best way to prepare not just one but hundreds of cases for trial?

Perhaps I'm overly naïve, or hardheaded, or both, because I did not give up. "Why?" I asked. "If we're all in the same boat and we're rowing in the same direction, who cares how we get the evidence as long as we get it?"

In an email, Berman's answer was simple: "I will be straight up," he wrote. "I don't want *Melton* to drive discovery."

Over the next year and a half, I learned that this was business as usual in a large MDL. The co-leads control everything and even try to put themselves into the middle of other attorneys' cases as a way of increasing their fees. They counted on GM at some point making a large settlement offer. The more you did leading up to that settlement, the more you were paid. Helping clients gave way to making a big financial score. I started to see every stereotype regarding personal injury attorneys play out right in front of my eyes. I did not care for it, nor did I plan to give in to it.

Berman and the other co-leads may have insisted they were running things, but they did not control the Melton case. Judge Tanksley had previously ordered GM to produce documents. Judge Furman's court did not supersede hers, although GM's attorney Richard Godfrey tried. Judge Furman brought in Judge Tanksley by speakerphone for part of the MDL hearings. The two of them had private conversations about the documents. I also made my case to her. My argument was simple. I told her that I should be able to request these documents as a part of representing Ken and Beth Melton in her court. Yes, I was a part of the federal litigation, but my primary responsibility was to my clients.

The September 27 deadline came without much sign of cooperation from GM or support from my co-leads. I kept pushing. I filed a motion to compel with Judge Tanksley. In spite of the co-leads' insistence, I refused to file a motion with Judge Furman. Doing so would have admitted he had authority over the Georgia state court. Judge Tanksley scheduled a hearing on my motion, which moved them to send many of the requested documents directly to us, as well as producing 4,123,346 pages of documents through the Everlaw program of the MDL. That was their way of refusing to admit that I was right. They also sent copies to Congress and NHTSA.

Technically I had prevailed, but it didn't feel like it. Either way, I had the documents I wanted. With those in hand, I began pushing to schedule depositions. The other side, which at times felt like it included my co-leads, wasn't about to let me win twice.

More of the Same

GM yielded on the question of documents before any court orders had to be issued. However, when it came to deposing witnesses, they were not about to compromise. All witnesses should be deposed only once, they argued, and those depositions had to be coordinated by Judge Furman's court. Elizabeth Cabraser, one of the co-leads, agreed. In an email to me and the other co-leads, she stated, "The ideal from a joint strategic standpoint would be to be able to say in this letter that depositions that assist the Melton trial preparation (including case-specific testimony) can be taken in the MDL, since the concealment issues cut across all cases, without irreparably delaying either the Melton trial or the commencement of depos in the MDL."

After lots of back-and-forth between me, the co-leads, and both courts, I had to yield on this point. While the co-leads assured me that they were trying to strike the right balance between *Melton* and the MDL, when it came to setting the schedule for depositions and leading the questioning of witnesses, that balance fell heavily toward the MDL. I went back to the fact that the co-leads received 3 percent of all settlements related to the MDL. Their insistence then made sense. This was their way of justifying the fees they expected to collect.

I hoped for the best, but even before the first deposition was taken, I became disillusioned. The co-leads requested, and Judge Furman granted, seven hours per deposition. I asked the co-leads what purpose this could possibly serve. These were videotaped depositions which would be played for the jury at trial. You do not have to have a sharp legal mind to understand that no jury can possibly sit through seven hours of testimony from one witness, much less witness after witness. I try to limit trial depositions to thirty minutes or less. Doing so demands that I think out all of my questions well in advance and go through them A, B, C, D, done.

When I raised these objections with the co-leads during a conference call, they made it clear they intended to take the full seven hours for each deposition.

"How is this going to work at trial?" I asked. "We all know jurors are going to lose interest after thirty minutes, much less seven hours."

"That's the way we're going to do it," I was informed, case closed.

As an olive branch, the co-leads told lawyers who had cases that were not in the MDL that they could have one hour to question witnesses after the co-leads asked their questions. Of course, these questions and answers were essentially useless since they took place after six hours of questioning, so that whatever favorable answer was obtained would be lost on the jurors. It was clear GM and its lawyers were pleased with the co-leads' deposition strategy.

On May 19, 2015, I attended the deposition of Jaclyn Palmer, a GM in-house lawyer who was assigned to *Melton* and other claims investigated before *Melton*. She was a crucial witness since she knew about the ignition switch defect and participated in the decision to settle cases and cover up the defect.

When I entered the large conference room at GM's headquarters at 400 Renaissance Center, 23rd Floor, Detroit, Michigan, I knew the fix was in. As a lawyer for the plaintiffs, I do not get paid until I obtain a financial recovery for my client. Time is money, and I don't have any of it to waste. That should have been the mindset in the MDL. We represented hundreds of cases with potentially thousands of clients. The point, I believed, was to get the testimony we needed to make our cases before a jury and win a judgment for our clients. I quickly learned that was not how the MDL deposition discovery process worked.

One of Hilliard's partners was at the Palmer deposition with multiple staff members, including lawyers and paralegals, all of whom meant more billable hours for the firm. I felt like I was back at the corporate firm in Orange County where I worked straight out of law school. The clock ran and the bill clicked higher and higher. The deposition went on and on and on. Hours of testimony, but nothing meaningful or helpful. In fact, the questioning gave Ms. Palmer the opportunity to explain herself and appear somewhat sympathetic. In the meantime, the clock ran and the bill clicked higher and higher.

But that wasn't the worst of it.

Mary Barra was scheduled to be deposed on October 19, 2015.

Her testimony could have been crucial to our case. When pressed in her Senate testimony about when she knew about the ignition switch defect, she feigned ignorance over and over again. Senator Boxer found Barra hard to believe, and so did I. I would have loved to have the chance to press her with the same line of questions.

However, I chose not to attend because I did not have a meaningful role in her questioning. Bob Hilliard chose to depose her himself. Reading her deposition transcript later, however, confirmed my worst fears about where this process was headed. Hilliard did not cross-examine her like a real attorney would do. He didn't go after her like he wanted to get past the wall of denial and dig down to the truth. Instead, he was so obsequious and deferential toward her that I started to wonder whose side he was on. To me, Hilliard came across as someone who wanted to placate the CEO of the corporation with whom he hoped to reach a favorable settlement soon. I found it disgusting how the litigation process had turned from holding a company accountable and compensating people for the harm done to them, to a bunch of lawyers figuring out how to get rich off of it.

Endgame

As all of this played out, Ken Feinberg contacted me to talk about settling the Melton case through his compensation fund. Because Brooke had died as a result of the ignition switch, our case fell under his authority if we chose to pursue it. Thus far, I had not seen a reason to do so. We had a very strong case and a trial date. However, with each passing day, I was becoming more and more frustrated with the way my hands had been tied by the MDL leadership. I had received the documents I'd requested, but I couldn't follow up on them through the deposition process.

By this point I had made up my mind not to attend any more depositions. Not one of them had produced anything more than billable hours for the attorneys and their teams taking them. Not even the deposition of Ray DeGiorgio produced any answers to the questions most pressing for the Melton case. I asked a few at the tail end of his seven hours in the witness stand, but he admitted nothing earth-shaking. While we still had a trial date, I felt less and less confident that taking this all the way to trial was going to be worth it for Ken and Beth.

Sometime in early 2015, Ken Feinberg called me again. "Lance, GM really wants to settle the Melton case. Do you think your clients would be interested?"

"I don't think so," I replied. "Besides, from what I know about your compensation plan, your parameters are too restrictive for this case, particularly on the compensation end of it."

"You need to seriously consider this. GM has given me the authority to treat the Melton case as extraordinary. I have the authority to decide how much to pay. Now, I have to take the numbers back to them for their final decision, but given the way the plan works, I feel very confident that GM will accept whatever I recommend."

"I'll talk to them and get back to you," I told Ken.

I then called Ken and Beth and had them come in to discuss the possibility of settling with GM a second time. I was honest with them. "We've done all we can do," I said. "They've given us all the documents we requested, and the evidence of what they did is out there. The federal MDL team is taking depositions, but they aren't helpful to us at all. Now all we can really do is sit here for a year and wait for our trial date."

We discussed the trial for a while, and how I felt about our chances of winning. "I don't really know," I admitted, "because my hands are tied. I cannot prepare the case the way I want to do it. On top of that, Ken Feinberg was clear that GM really wants to settle this case." I explained how GM wanted to put all of this behind them as quickly as possible. Every day that Cobalt ignition switches showed up in the news was one day more that they'd have to wait to fully rebuild their public image.

"So what do you think we should do?" Ken asked.

"Normally, I'd say let's keep fighting, but now I'm not so sure we should. They recalled 30 million cars last year, thanks to you. The truth about how they covered up a defective product even as it caused fatalities is also out there. Most of the lies they told to us have also been revealed. I'd say in terms of what we hoped to accomplish, we don't have anything left to prove.

"Now, we can still go to trial, and I'd say our chances are really, really good. When we refiled, our goal was punitive damages. GM just paid a $900 million fine to the federal government. Again, they recalled close to 30 million vehicles. They can certainly appeal to the jury that they have been punished and have been, and are, doing the right thing. A jury may not be in the mood to add to it. They might say GM has paid the price. While you and I may not agree with that, that's just the reality of how people will see it. Even if we do win and the jury comes back and tacks on punitive damages to the wrongful death judgment, GM will turn around and appeal it, which is going to tack on another three or four years," I said.

When I mentioned three or four years, Beth's head dropped.

"I know. I don't want that either," I said.

"What are our options, then?" Ken asked.

A long discussion ensued, but not about the money. The three of us wanted to see GM go before a jury and answer for what they had done. Yes, GM commissioned the Valukas report, but when you read it closely, you can see it does more to repair GM's image than find fault with the core of what they did in this case. And while they had paid a substantial fine and had compensated victims through the Feinberg fund, that still didn't feel like justice.

Finally, I said, "I don't want to go through mediation or do the usual settlement process. The two of you don't need that. Let's agree on a number that it will take to settle this, and I'll call Ken and see what he says."

The three of us discussed a number, which remains confidential. Suffice it to say, I thought it was a number they would never agree to pay. I called Ken and said, "This is the number. If you recommend it to GM and they accept it, then the case will be over."

Ken balked when he heard the number. "That's way too high," he said, "more than GM would ever expect to pay, even in the Melton case."

"Well, Ken, that's our number. We aren't coming down. This isn't open to negotiation," I said.

"Okay. Let me talk it over with them and I'll let you know what they say," Ken replied.

A day or two later, Ken called me back and said, "I have persuaded GM to accept that number."

I immediately called Ken and Beth. "They said yes. It's over. You won," I said. GM's nightmare from us was over.

As part of our settlement with GM, they asked us to settle with Thornton Chevrolet as quickly as possible. However, that was not entirely up to us. Thus far, Thornton's attorney, who actually worked for their insurance company, had dug in their heels and refused to budge from the lowball offer they made at our first attempt at mediation. I did not expect that to change now. If anything, I thought the fact that we had settled with GM for a confidential amount of money would make them even more obstinate.

However, a short time after I reached an agreement with Ken Feinberg on behalf of GM, Thornton's attorney called me asking what it would take to settle the case now. We reached an agreement rather quickly for far more than they had said Thornton would ever pay. I am not sure what changed their mind, but I have always wondered if perhaps GM helped Thornton see the case in a different light. Either way, the Thornton part of the case was also over. There would be no trial. The case was finished.

I guess this chapter should have a happier tone. Technically, we won. Ken and Beth received an unprecedented settlement. Yet at the moment, I didn't feel like celebrating. I had already seen the writing on the wall with the way the MDL was going. GM had the federal case under control. Of course they were going to pay out another huge settlement to make it all go away, but that was just the price of doing business for them. The most important thing for them was they now controlled the process because they had the main MDL attorneys under control. No one in leadership wanted to rock the boat. No one wanted a pound of flesh from GM that might leave the automaker reeling for years to come. They all wanted to make nice until the settlement came and everyone walked away with a nice payday. I couldn't stomach it any longer, yet somehow, things grew worse.

CHAPTER 20

The End . . . for Me

Never in my worst nightmares did I expect to read the January 22, 2016, headline: "GM Wins Big in First Trial over Deadly Ignition Switch," but after all that had happened over the previous year, it didn't surprise me. In fact, I predicted the result. I, however, took no satisfaction in being right. I fully expected it even though it should have been impossible.

Between what we had uncovered in *Melton* and all of the evidence disclosed in the more than four million pages of documents GM produced since the Valukas report's release, an ignition switch trial never should have been lost. That's why GM was eager to settle most before they ever went to trial. They were very eager to put all this behind them. Even though GM admitted these ignition switches were defective, a plaintiff would still have to convince a jury that the defect caused the injuries. Any case that went to trial had to have this proof, which takes me back to the headline of January 22, 2016.

The Bellwether Process

Even though so many cases settled or people accepted compensation through the Feinberg compensation fund, cases still remained in the MDL. Through my work on the executive committee, I was very familiar with many of the cases. Some were strong. As part of the MDL process, the judge schedules "bellwether" trials, whose outcomes serve as an indicator of how juries will respond to the evidence presented. That gives both sides a good indication of what it will take to settle the cases. If the juries in the bellwether trials come back with a substantial verdict for the plaintiffs, then the settlement offers from the defendants go up. But if the juries come back with a smaller than expected award for the plaintiffs, or if they rule for the defendant, any remaining plaintiffs will probably have to take less to settle their cases. That's why they're called bellwether. They give everyone a good idea of the value of the cases.

Judge Furman decided that our MDL would have six bellwether trials. He gave our side the opportunity to pick the first, third, and fifth cases to go to trial, while GM chose the second, fourth, and sixth. Because these trials set the tone for every other case, ideally the plaintiffs choose their strongest case to kick off the bellwether process, with the second strongest as the third and the third strongest the last of the bellwether trials. As the defendant, GM naturally would pick what they perceived to be the weakest for the second, fourth, and sixth. That allows everything to balance out and gives an accurate picture of the overall strength of the MDL cases.

If every attorney with a case in the MDL did a good job of screening their clients, all the cases should be strong, even the weakest of them all. By this point we had 124 confirmed fatalities from ignition switch related accidents (or ten times the number GM had grudgingly admitted in the Valukas report), along with 275 people injured. The gap between GM's numbers and what we could conservatively prove showed the overall strength of the cases against GM. Based on the evidence, the plaintiffs should have easily won all six bellwether trials, even those GM chose. The only real question should have been the size of the jury awards.

Unfortunately, the GM ignition switch MDL was less than ideal. It was filled with cases that never should have been filed. No attorney had more bad cases in the MDL than Bob Hilliard. His boast of the hundreds of cases that landed him his position as a co-lead now came back to blow up in our faces. Hilliard had signed up anyone who claimed to have been injured in a General Motors product without thoroughly vetting their claims. While that presented enough of a problem, it compounded itself when he insisted on placing his cases in the bellwether trials.

All MDL plaintiffs had an interest in making sure the initial bellwether cases were as strong as possible for the plaintiffs. One of our expert witnesses in the ignition switch litigation, Professor Charles Silver, from the University of Texas, said it best: "The single greatest source of bargaining leverage a plaintiff's attorney has in settlement negotiations is the threat of winning at trial and forcing the defendant to pay a price set by a jury . . . The most important task for any plaintiff's attorney is to convince a defendant that if it takes a case to trial, it will get creamed."

Unfortunately, five of the six cases that were ultimately chosen as the first group of bellwether trials were Hilliard's cases, including the GM selections. By that time, GM knew each of Hilliard's cases was a strong defense case, meaning that there was little proof that the ignition switch defect caused the injuries claimed by his clients. In addition, his clients were not seriously injured. Obviously, the three cases filed by him and chosen by GM were considered to be the worst cases since they were selected by GM. The two selections by Hilliard were weak cases as well. The bellwether selection process only reinforced my concerns about Hilliard. From the start of the MDL, he came across to me as one more interested in having power and control, and therefore getting a larger piece of the pie when GM started writing checks, than in doing what was best for the clients.

Fortunately, the first bellwether case selected for trial, *Yingling v. GM*, was not one of Hilliard's. The case centered on an accident that took place between the time GM had decided to recall all cars with the faulty switch and the actual announcement of the decision. That fact made this case even more egregious. On November 21, 2013,

James Yingling, a thirty-five-year-old father of five, lost control of his 2006 Saturn Ion when his ignition switch dropped from run to accessory. His car went off the road and into a ditch, where it crashed into a concrete culvert. The airbags did not deploy. Yingling suffered a traumatic brain injury from which he died two weeks after the accident. Given the timing of the accident, this should have been the perfect case for GM to get creamed.

The jury, however, did not get the opportunity to hear it. Before the co-leads selected the Yingling case to be the first bellwether trial, one of Hilliard's partners in his firm contacted the lead attorney for the Yingling family, Victor Pribanic. Hilliard's partner informed Pribanic that his case stood a better chance of being chosen as the first bellwether if Pribanic would agree to have Hilliard and his firm come in on the case and split the fees 50/50. Of course, Pribanic declined.

Shortly before the bellwether trial schedule was set, Hilliard himself called Pribanic and informed him he was considering selecting *Yingling* as the first bellwether trial. He also expressed an interest in trying the case with Mr. Pribanic. When Pribanic said he'd never considered that, Hilliard said he'd fly out to Pittsburgh so that the two of them could talk it over. The co-leads did indeed select *Yingling* as the first bellwether trial. A few days later, on July 30, 2015, Hilliard flew out to Pittsburgh for a dinner meeting with Pribanic. The subject of trying the case together never came up. Two days later, however, Hilliard called again to discuss how they might split the attorneys' fees if they tried the case together. Hilliard offered to allow Pribanic to keep all of the fees if he settled before going to trial. If the case went all the way to trial, however, they needed some arrangement for dividing the fee. Hilliard's intentions were clear. If *Yingling* was going to remain the first bellwether trial, Hilliard needed a piece of the action.

Hilliard's actions were greedy and unethical. To even suggest that another attorney split their fees with him should have been grounds for Hilliard's immediate removal as a co-lead. While the co-leads stand in the shoes of all the MDL plaintiffs' lawyers through the discovery process, once a case goes to trial, the co-leads offer assistance but should defer to the lawyer who represents the bellwether client. For Hilliard to even think that he should somehow profit from another attorney's case violates the purpose of an MDL. Co-leads have a duty, according to the codes governing such things, to act fairly, efficiently, and economically in the interests of all parties and parties' counsel. Instead, Hilliard did just the opposite.

On August 3, Pribanic sent a letter to Hilliard, politely declining his offer. Two days later, on August 5, 2015, without notice to the executive committee or any other plaintiffs' counsel, the co-leads sent a letter to Judge Furman requesting they modify the bellwether trial schedule. Rather than being the lead, *Yingling* was now relegated to the fifth trial. In its place, the co-leads chose one of Hilliard's cases, with another of his as the third. GM also chose three of Hilliard's cases as bellwether trials, giving him five of the six.

Before any of this happened, I stepped away from the MDL. I'd already had enough. However, I did not publicly resign from my position on the executive committee because I knew the press would have a field day with that decision. Instead I informed the co-leads that I could not continue with the direction they were taking the MDL. Other attorneys told me I was crazy. The co-leads told me I should stick with it, help out where I could, and keep close time sheets so that I could bill all the time I had invested once a settlement was reached. I told them that's not how I did business and that I had plenty of other cases to keep me busy.

Even though I had stepped aside from actively working in the MDL, I kept up with what was going on inside of it. When the co-leads selected the first bellwether trial, I knew I had made the right decision. I reviewed the documents describing the accident and the alleged injuries. It did not take me long to realize that if it went to trial, it would be a disaster for all plaintiffs. Robert Scheuer of Oklahoma crashed his 2003 Saturn Ion into a tree in May 2014, or three months after GM recalled it to repair the ignition switch. Scheuer claimed his airbags did not deploy. Although his injuries proved to be minor, he claimed he suffered memory loss which caused him to misplace a large check for the down payment on his dream home.

Unlike the Yingling case or Brooke's accident, Hilliard did not have SDM data showing the car had switched from run to accessory. Hilliard didn't even have the car to prove whether the airbags had deployed. Somehow the vehicle had not been preserved even though Scheuer knew he might have a potential claim against GM. Scheuer's injuries were also minor. Taken together, all of this made for a very weak first case to take to a jury. No lawyer, other than perhaps one representing GM, would want to try *Scheuer* before *Yingling,* but the co-leads decided otherwise. To me, there was only one explanation for their actions. They wanted to make sure one of their cases led off the bellwether process so that they could maximize their financial position in the MDL in the process. The merits of the first case mattered less than who controlled it. Months before the case went to trial, I knew there was a good chance it would go poorly. For at least three months, I fired off email after email warning that this case was a disaster waiting to happen, but no one listened. Not even I imagined the trial could go as badly as it did.

Worst-Case Scenario

The Scheuer bellwether trial began on January 12, 2016. I did not attend or even follow it on television. Sonja and I went to Liberia on a mission trip while the trial was going on. Even from the other side of the world, I knew what was coming.

Steve Berman joined Bob Hilliard in representing Scheuer. As the first bellwether trial against GM, the case drew a great deal of media attention. A few days into the trial, a new bombshell dropped. Robert Scheuer testified about how his injuries caused him to be evicted from his dream home. The real estate agent who sold Scheuer and his wife their home heard about Scheuer's testimony on the radio. He immediately contacted GM's legal team with a different version of how the eviction played out. As it turns out, Scheuer was evicted because he forged a document he used to buy his house. Investigators found Scheuer had altered a government check stub for proof of income, changing it from $430.72 to $441,430.72. The real estate agent also showed that Scheuer went away on vacation shortly after the crash even though he claimed he was bedridden from his injuries during that time.

Needless to say, this bombshell blew the trial out of the water. Judge Furman dismissed the jury before hearing evidence of Scheuer's fraud. After hearing the new evidence, Furman urged both sides to end the trial and move on to the second bellwether, which was set for March. To no one's surprise, Scheuer agreed to drop his case with prejudice, which means he can never refile it. He also agreed to take no payment from GM for his claims. Of course, Hilliard and Berman tried to put on a good front. Hilliard called the development unexpected and stunning. Rather than admit he and the other co-leads chose a poor case to use as the first bellwether, he claimed that regardless of how this case turned out, the airbags still did not deploy, which made it a good representation of the rest of the cases in the MDL.

When I heard about what happened, I emailed another attorney and said only Bob Hilliard could turn an iron-clad fraud case against GM into a case where GM could allege fraud. It was a disaster for the remaining cases in the MDL, but a gift to GM. Now they appeared to be the victim of greedy people who were trying to scam them and get something for nothing. From a PR standpoint, the first trial could not have gone any better for General Motors.

The second bellwether trial didn't go much better. Dionne Spain and Lawrence Barthelemy of New Orleans, also clients of Bob Hilliard, claimed they lost control of their 2007 Saturn Sky on a bridge and crashed when the ignition switch inadvertently turned to accessory. However, the accident occurred on an icy bridge where thirty-eight other accidents took place on the same night. All of the other thirty-eight blamed a run of black ice that covered the bridge. Unlike the first trial, this one went all the way to the jury. Jurors took less than a day to determine that the switch made the Saturn Sky unreasonably dangerous and that GM had failed to warn customers about its safety risk. However, they also found that icy conditions and not the ignition switch caused the accident. Therefore, the jury awarded Spain and Barthelemy no damages. GM was now two for two in the bellwether trials. This was beyond a disaster. Something needed to be done.

Motion to Dismiss

I didn't wait for the second bellwether trial to do something I wished I'd done months earlier. I was still in Liberia on my mission trip when I called Doreen and told her it was time to get to work. Over the next three evenings, I dictated a motion to Doreen that I wanted filed as soon as possible. On January 25, 2016, four days after the *Scheuer* disaster, Doreen filed in Judge Furman's court a motion to remove the co-leads and reconsider the bellwether trial schedule. Before we filed, I emailed other attorneys who still had cases in the MDL, but most didn't want to join me. Only nine did. I understood why most people turned me down. They hoped to be a part of another MDL at some point in the future, and rocking the boat with Berman, Hilliard, and Cabraser might hurt their chances of doing that.

My motion was blistering, maybe too much so, but I did not care at the time. I opened by writing, "This is no easy motion. But it is the right motion. It has to be made. And it is made for the benefit of all plaintiffs who are part of this Multidistrict Litigation." I went on to chronicle the things I've included in the last few chapters. I showed how the co-leads had mismanaged this litigation from the outset. Rather than coordinate with the other lawyers in the MDL, the co-leads worked with the GM lawyers to make sure all other firms were essentially frozen out from all strategic and tactical decisions regarding the discovery process. I didn't pull any punches when it came to what I believed to be the first priority of the co-leads. I wrote, "Over time it became clear that the prosecution of the case was not about obtaining the necessary evidence to present the best case at trial. Rather, it was about billing hours and carving out hours and making sure the co-leads controlled this process. In short, it was about making money for the co-leads." Unsurprisingly, the co-leads disagreed with what I'd said. They also sent an email to the other MDL lawyers praising their effectiveness, presumably in an effort to reassure everyone that the MDL was in good hands.

I did not expect Judge Furman to grant my motion, and I was correct. In dismissing my motion, he basically told me I was Monday-morning quarterbacking by questioning after the fact the decisions that went into selecting *Scheuer* as the first bellwether trial. In response I produced six months of emails showing I said the same things long before *Scheuer* ended in disaster. Not that it mattered. He denied my motion and I officially removed myself from the MDL leadership. When the story hit the press, most reported it as a squabble between attorneys. Some accused me of sour grapes, saying I wanted to replace the co-leads myself. Nothing could be farther from the truth. I didn't want the job. I just wanted someone in there who was more interested in the needs of the clients than in lining his own pockets.

Behind the scenes, things were quite different. The attorneys who did not want to join me in sticking my neck out in filing the motion emailed me later thanking me for bringing this ugliness to light. I still had about a hundred cases in conjunction with Beasley Allen pending with GM. Shortly after I filed my motion, they approached us about settling them. Over the next few months we negotiated settlements on every one. GM also settled the Yingling case before it could go to trial. No other cases have gone to trial since the two disastrous bellwether trials. Basically, it was now over. At least it was over for me. And the damage was over for GM. Even the headlines of the two bellwether trials did not register with the public as the faulty switch headlines once had. Not long after *Scheuer*, the 2016 presidential primaries were in full swing. Americans have a short attention span at the best of times. By the time of the November general election, even the memory of the Cobalt cover-up had begun to fade. For everyone involved, it was back to business as usual, especially for GM.

CHAPTER 21

A Happy Ending?

I guess we won, but in the immediate aftermath of walking away from the MDL once and for all, it didn't feel like it. In the spring and summer of 2014, we had GM on the ropes. Between the recalls and Mary Barra's testimony before Congress and the daily negative press, the company was reeling. I planned to keep pushing. I did not want them to go out of business; I simply wanted them to accept full responsibility for what they had done. Some say they did just that with the Valukas report and the Feinberg compensation fund, but I disagree. GM did both of those because they could not survive otherwise.

And while the compensation fund approved $600 million in payments for 124 deaths, eighteen cases of brain damage, amputations, quadriplegia, paraplegia, or severe burns, and 248 hospitalizations, it also rejected another 3,952 cases as deficient or ineligible. Multiple other settlements took place outside of the compensation fund. All told, GM paid out at least $2.5 billion in fines and settlement costs, and yet they still found a way to rewrite the narrative. The Scheuer trial transformed them from perpetrators of a fraud to a victim of unscrupulous opportunists who saw GM's downfall as a means to make a quick buck. Taken together with the general perception that they fell on their sword with Valukas and Feinberg, the reshaping of their public image was complete.

The results were easy to see. Two years after recalling 30 million cars, GM sold a record 10 million vehicles worldwide and reported a profit of $12.5 billion, which was also a record. Even though GM paid a $900 million fine to settle criminal charges with the justice department, no individual was ever charged with a crime. No one went to jail for negligent homicide. Instead, *Fortune* magazine named Mary Barra the world's most powerful woman of 2016. The next year *Barron's* listed her as one of the most influential CEOs in the world because of how quickly she led GM's recovery from the ignition switch disaster. It was as though Brooke Melton's death and those of more than a hundred others melted away from the public consciousness. Today, the entire Cobalt cover-up feels like a distant memory, which was GM's plan.

And yet we still won. More accurately, the civil justice system won. Even with the abuses I confronted during the MDL, and even with a handful of unethical personal injury lawyers abusing the system by signing up anyone and everyone regardless of whether they had a case, the system still worked the way it is supposed to work. The civil justice system holds companies accountable in ways that government oversight never will. The Cobalt ignition switch is a perfect example of this. The National Highway Traffic Safety Administration is supposed to oversee automobile manufacturers. Any safety defect must be reported to them within five days of discovery. Even if a company fails to self-report, when anyone makes NHTSA aware of a safety problem, the agency is supposed to investigate.

That's exactly what they did with the Cobalt switch. NHTSA launched their first investigation into the problem of engine stalls with GM products in 2004. Later, in March 2007, NHTSA officials informed GM they'd received numerous reports of airbag nondeployments with the Cobalt. Yet both times, NHTSA did nothing. Given the way in which government officials jump to jobs within the very industries they are supposed to oversee, then back again, it's not surprising. The foxes truly are watching the henhouse.

That is why the civil justice system is an essential check to corporate power. I own my own business. I believe in capitalism as much as the next guy. Yet left unrestrained, companies will do whatever they can get away with. It's human nature. As a Christ follower, I understand the fallen nature of mankind. The Bible calls it our sin nature. John Calvin referred to it as the total depravity of man. Depravity does not end with the individual. It infects everything human beings touch and create. In a corporate setting, mankind's essential depravity reveals itself in a culture that puts profit ahead of human life and then shirks all responsibility with things like the GM nod and salute.

Though far from perfect, the civil justice system brings such actions to light. Through the work of Doreen Lundrigan, Charlie Miller, and Mark Hood, we discovered the faulty ignition switch. During the process of discovery, we uncovered the fact that GM knew the switch did not meet their minimum torque specifications even before they authorized its use first in the Saturn Ion and later the Cobalt and other vehicles. Our team also discovered they had in fact changed the part to meet specifications in the 2007 model year, yet covered their tracks by not changing the part number. Our efforts ultimately led to the recalls, Senate hearings, criminal charges, class action suits, and the MDL. In a word, our lawsuit held GM's feet to the fire. Even though I would have loved to take them even farther and bring the case before a jury, at the end of the day, we brought to light a deadly secret that may well never have been fully revealed otherwise.

As much as we accomplished, I wanted to do more, but that wasn't possible. Ecclesiastes 7:13 says, "Accept the way God does things, for who can straighten what he has made crooked?" (NLT). Life is crooked. Life is messy. Bad things happen, and although we stand up against them, our efforts are limited in this fallen world. Try as we might to make sense of why God allows these things to happen, we simply cannot. Yet I found a beauty in this crookedness of life. The path down which he took me through this journey went any direction but straight. In the beginning, I never imagined this case might unfold as it did. All along the way, I found I had to constantly check my heart and examine my motivation for moving forward.

I found this to be especially true when the case came out of the shadows and landed on the front page of the business section of *USA Today* and in the halls of Congress. It was easy to allow my head to swell and take more credit than I was due. During those four or five months of intense media frenzy in the spring and summer of 2014, Sonja and I had many long conversations between the two of us and with our children about how we could not allow ourselves to get caught up in all of this. "This will come and go," Sonja reminded us. "How we handle this is what is going to last." Believe me, it was not easy. Marietta is not that large of a community. Everywhere we went, people mentioned seeing me on the news or reading about me in the paper. I had to continually remind myself that none of this was about me. God had placed me in this position not to promote myself but to seek justice for Brooke Melton and the others I represented who had been injured or killed.

Whenever someone praised me for my work, I thought back to a grandmother who lost control of her Cobalt because of the ignition switch. She survived the accident, but her grandson did not. The guilt of thinking she had caused this precious child's death nearly overwhelmed her. To be able to tell her that the accident was not her fault and that we were going to hold those responsible accountable was why I was in this position. That was my purpose, not to make a name for myself.

As I wrote in the preface, I know God brought the Meltons to my office. Using me to uncover what GM had hidden and finding some measure of justice for Ken and Beth and others, that was all his idea, not mine. Looking back at the case, I cannot say I or my team did anything out of the ordinary. The case was extraordinary, not us. We prosecuted the case just as we always do. The facts of the case caused it to grow in importance, not anything we did. To be honest, my first inclination was to pass on the case. I didn't think there was anything I could do to help Ken and Beth. God took it from there.

That is not to say I conducted myself perfectly throughout every step. The MDL pushed my patience, and my Christian walk, to the limits. Looking back, there are several things I wish I'd done differently, but confronting the co-leads is not one of those things. I wish only that I'd done that sooner, not that the results would have been different. At times I find myself wishing I'd asked to be one of the co-leads rather than a member of the executive committee. Perhaps if I'd been in that position, I might have been able to exert greater influence over the bellwether process as well as keep the focus on the clients rather than the money to be made in any future settlement. The odds of my effecting a different outcome would have depended on who filled the other two positions. If Bob Hilliard and Steve Berman had been my co-leads, the end probably would have been even messier than it was.

Some days I wish I'd never become involved beyond the Melton case. If I had not been a part of any of the MDL suits, then I could have maintained my independence as I pursued the second Melton suit without interference. Hindsight is always 20/20, but that course would have allowed me to prepare the case the way I wanted and to take it all the way to trial. Even though I feel very confident we would have won, the result for the Meltons may not have been any different than the settlement we were able to negotiate. I also think it was probably best for my clients to end this when we did rather than drag it out for years. They had suffered far too much, and their contribution to holding GM accountable went far beyond what anyone could be expected to give. Even so, I sometimes wonder what a jury would have done to GM. But that was not to be. Justice was still served as God brought that which was hidden out into the light.

And this truly was a work of God. Now that the case is a couple of years in my rearview mirror, I feel an overwhelming sense of gratitude to him that he entrusted this case to me. Opportunities like this are rare. Never did I expect to be thrust into such a glaring spotlight. My prayer then, and my prayer now, is that my conduct and my attitude honored my God.

Francis Schaeffer once penned an essay called "No Little People, No Little Places." His closing words reflect my feelings as I consider how God used me in the Melton case. Schaeffer wrote, "As we get on a bit in our lives, knowing how weak we are, if we look back and see we have been somewhat used of God, then we should be the rod 'surprised by joy.'"[15] That is exactly how I feel. I am truly surprised by joy.

ACKNOWLEDGMENTS

There is no book without a Melton case, and there is no Melton case but for the remarkable efforts of others.

First and foremost, I must acknowledge my wife, Sonja. Without her support, none of this ever would have happened. Who she is allows me to do what I do.

Next, Ken and Beth are the true heroes of this story. Their perseverance in the face of overwhelming odds not only honored Brooke, it no doubt saved lives.

Doreen Lundrigan's invaluable contributions must also be recognized. Doreen personifies our firm's motto, "Relentlessly pursuing justice." Because of her relentlessness, we were able to discover the "smoking guns" GM had hidden for years. Doreen treats every case just like the Melton case. Her pursuit of justice for each of our clients for almost twenty years now is not only unique, it is inspirational.

I must also acknowledge Mark Hood and Charlie Miller. I have no doubt God providentially introduced me to Mark and Charlie. I have worked with numerous experts over the years, but had never worked with them. Furthermore, Mark was assigned to this case because the CEO engineer was too busy to work on it. Mark was the perfect man for the job. His dogged persistence cracked the case wide open.

And then there is Charlie. Without Charlie we would not have learned of the evidence which showed GM knew of the ignition-switch defect before GM sold the Cobalt to Brooke. Also, without Charlie I would not have been introduced to Mark. Simply put, Charlie Miller was the finest expert I have ever worked with.

Sadly, Charlie passed away on August 25, 2019. He died at his beloved hunting club in Merigold, Mississippi. True to his humble Mississippi Delta roots, Charlie's obituary says, "He was a forensic-mechanic expert witness for the last twenty-five years." No mention of his role in *Melton* or the other important cases he worked on. Typical Charlie. Thank you, Charlie, and God be with you.

Finally, I want to thank Mark Tabb for his invaluable assistance in writing this book. I write legal briefs for a living and never thought writing a book would be so difficult. Believe me, it is. Mark, however, made a difficult process enjoyable, and for that I am truly grateful.

NOTES

1. Jeff Sabatini, "Making a Case for Ignitions That Don't Need Keys," *New York Times*, June 19, 2005.
2. Gary Heller, "All New Cobalt Has Good, Bad Points," *The Daily Item*, May 26, 2005.
3. Christopher Jensen, "Salamis, Key Rings and GM's Ongoing Sense of Humor," *The Plain Dealer*, June 26, 2005.
4. Valukas report, 204.
5. Ibid., 255.
6. Ibid., 256.
7. Bill Vlasic, "G.M. Inquiry Cites Years of Neglect over Fatal Defect," *New York Times*, June 5, 2014.
8. Valukas report, 2, emphasis added.
9. Ibid., 3–4.
10. Ibid., 211.
11. Ibid., 162.
12. Ibid., 162–63, emphasis added.
13. Alex Taylor III, "How One Rogue Employee Can Upend a Whole Company," *Fortune*, June 11, 2014.
14. Valukas report, 48.
15. Francis Schaeffer, "Book One: No Little People," in *The Complete Works of Francis Schaeffer*, vol. 3, *A Christian View of Spirituality* (Westchester, IL: Crossway, 1982), 11.